Winning in the Trust & Value Economy

Winning in the Trust and Value Economy

A Guide to Sales Success and Business Growth

MERIDITH ELLIOTT POWELL

GLOBAL
professional
publishing

Global Professional Publishing Ltd
Random Acres
Slip Mill Lane
Hawkhurst
Cranbrook
Kent TN18 5AD
Email: publishing@gppbooks.com

ISBN 978-1-906403-966

Printed in the United States by Integrated Book Technology

**For full details of Global Professional Publishing titles in
Finance, Banking and Management see our website at:
www.gppbooks.com**

Contents

Foreword

When Meridith asked me to write the Foreword for her latest book: *Winning in the Trust and Value Economy*, I was both thrilled and honored.

I have had the pleasure of working with Meridith on my podcast— *The Ambitious Entrepreneur Show*—where she regularly shared her expansive leadership and business development insights with my podcast community. Her wealth of knowledge, particularly on the topic of how to convert prospects into customers easily and authentically in a changing economy, is incredible.

Meridith is one of those rare people who walks her talk: she is an exceptional leader and example in how we can nurture relationships, add immense value, build trust, remain at the forefront of business trends, while embracing innovation and driving change to ensure we not only survive, but can thrive in this new economy.

You have taken a powerful step forward in your business just by having picked up this book. Now, by reading and implementing the practical, how-to steps that Meridith shares in her latest book, you will ensure you can step out confidently and 'win' in this new trust and value economy. Are you ready?!

Annemarie Cross

Annemarie Cross is a Business Coach & Marketing Mentor for ambitious entrepreneurs and the Founder and CEO of The Ambitious Entrepreneur Podcast Network. www.AmbitiousEntrepreneurNetwork.com

didn't want to look, but you couldn't help yourself. It was nothing if not fascinating and depressing all at the same time.

Then up out of the ashes came this new group of businesses, this group of organizations that were somehow finding success. Stories of their success were few and far between. But if you paid close attention to the news, the rare story about a company actually doing well would pop up.

It began to look to me as if there was a group of business leaders and professionals who belonged to a secret club. A group who had figured this economy out. By the close of 2011, I found myself observing and then actually being lucky enough to work with companies that were not only finding success but were on course to have their best years on record. They were experiencing record growth, attracting new clients, recruiting fantastic talent and building strong bench. They actually seemed to be enjoying this economy.

I was amazed and eager to learn more. Here we were as a country facing some of the toughest economic challenges we had ever faced, where people were out of work, the mortgage industry in crisis, bankruptcies at an all time high, and companies with a long history of success going under. Yet, in the face of all this doom and gloom, there were organizations posting record years and celebrating growth rates of 30 and 40 percent. I had to know why. I had to understand exactly what these companies were doing differently and why what they were doing was not only keeping them profitable in this economy but allowing them to reach all-time highs.

So I asked.

I set up interviews with the CEOs of these flourishing companies and their team members—those people working in the front-line trenches of this economy and thriving. What I learned was fascinating, fresh and different. All of these people were so open, so honest, so motivating and inspiring to talk with that I knew their information, ideas and strategies simply had to be shared with more people than me. And that is how *Winning in the Trust and Value Economy: A Guide to Sales Success and Business Growth* came to be.

This book is based on the insights, information and tactics I gained from spending time with and learning from these CEOs and their teams. I learned how they view this economy, and the steps they took to turn their organizations around, navigate this new world and achieve in shifting economic times.

These innovative leaders have cracked the code to finding success and opportunity in this uncertain economy. They shared that code with me. And now I'm sharing it with you.

In fact, I thought that what they told me was so revolutionary that I decided this new economy needed its own name. So I christened it the Trust & Value Economy. The name suits it because "trust and value" are what this economy is all about—building and developing both with yourself, your employees and your customers. As business owners, professionals and team members, we all need to understand that times have changed and business is never going back to the way it was, no matter how healthy the economy gets.

Just think about it, just think about how much has changed: globalization, increased competition and advances in technology. How many of us are using the same computer or telephone or watching the same television we did five years ago? How often do you pick up *The Wall Street Journal* or *Inc. Magazine* and find articles about outsourcing, companies expanding into India and China, or young entrepreneurs in third-world countries. And five years ago,

4

who would have thought that your retail bookstore or shoestore would consider companies on the Internet or in remote towns or in far-off corners of the world as major competition? Yes, times and the business landscape have seriously changed.

And that's what this new economy is all about—change. It is chaotic, and all signs point to it continuing to be that way. In my lifetime, I have never known an economy like this. And I have to tell you, I am excited about it.

Yes, there are challenges. And it demands that we get comfortable with the unknown, and that, quite frankly, is uncomfortable and a little scary. But there are so many upsides to this economy, so much opportunity for business owners and sales professionals. If you are willing to work, if you are willing to commit to innovation, if you are willing to take a little risk and be open to new ideas and strategies, this is your economy. For the first time, as far back as I can remember, we are living in economic times when transparency, authenticity and truly doing the right thing not only pay off but are the only ways to truly thrive.

One thing to keep in mind as you read this book and begin to learn the strategies, tips and actions that will move your business forward in this new age is that there is no magic bullet. While today, hard work alone will not get you where you want to go, it is still required. The one belief that every key leader in this book shared was that success still takes a great deal of effort. While they are working differently, more smartly and with a whole new approach, it is still hard work. If you want to succeed, you have to be willing to put in the time and some good old-fashioned elbow grease.

So welcome to the Trust & Value Economy, and welcome to *Winning in the Trust and Value Economy: A Guide to Sales Success and*

Business Growth. This book contains the information you need to make this economy work for you.

In the first few chapters, you'll learn how this economy has changed and how the consumer has changed. You'll discover why this economy is different, and what you need to do to not only accept but embrace that change.

As you dig deeper into each chapter, you'll uncover the insights, strategies and wisdom that business leaders have shared about what they are doing to reshape their cultures, develop their employees, redefine their marketing strategies and assure the overall success of their companies. The book also reveals what today's leader looks like, and why courage and humility are the traits needed most by today's executives.

Additionally, what you will gain from this book is the knowledge that there is no one way and no certainty in the Trust & Value Economy. And whether you are in charge of or represent a company, you have to find comfort and confidence in your ability to be successful in the middle of complete chaos. But when you learn what the Trust & Value Economy is really asking of business and take the time to instill that in every member of your team and every part of your process, success amid chaos is not as hard as it sounds.

After all I've witnessed in the last few years, I know this is an economy in which you can be successful, one in which you can win. Believe me when I say, this is *your* economy. And after reading this book, you will be more than prepared to go out there and succeed like never before.

CHAPTER 1

The Economic Shift—It's A Good Thing

Unless you live in a bubble, completely isolated from the media, you have undoubtedly been bombarded with the seemingly endless stream of negative economic news and predictions for years now. With each new corporate collapse, slight dip in the stock market, government bailout, increase in national debt or mortgage crisis, the entire world seems ever more fixated on what has gone wrong and offers only pessimistic assumptions that we are doomed to stay in a place of hopeless economic depression forever.

We are hard pressed these days to turn on the news, glance at a newspaper or even eavesdrop at the grocery store without reading or hearing about the disaster that is the economy. We hear reports about how the economy is shrinking, the ever-depressing unemployment rates, and the constant speculation of when things are going to "turn around." Honestly, it's like one long, bad reality show.

The economy has shifted—and it's not shifting back

Well, I am here to put an end to the speculation for you. I am here to tell you that things are not going to turn around. Yes, you heard me right. Things are not going to turn around. Sounds harsh? A little depressing? Maybe. But what's more depressing is the thought that if you are waiting to make a move once this economy "bounces back," you are going to be sitting still for a long time.

And sitting still in this economy is moving backwards.

This economy is never going to "bounce back" to the way it was. Why? Because this economy is not just down, as many claim; it has changed, and changed forever. A new economy has taken its place. An economy that I'm calling the Trust & Value Economy. And that's the good news.

Before this whole economic shift started, back before the economic downturn ushered in this new economic reality, we were in what I would call a "product and service" economy. A business provided a product or service, consumers bought or didn't buy what the business offered. And that was that. The customer may always

8

have been right, but the business was in control of what was available for purchase and where and when it could be bought. Buying was more about convenience and price. We had the luxury of taking our customers for granted. Where else were they going to go? For the majority of transactions, customers were limited by proximity to the goods and services.

A case in point, in my hometown, Asheville, North Carolina. We have a legendary shoe store, Tops for Shoes. The store takes up half a city block. The selection is unbelievable. You can find any type of shoe—from hiking to formal, in any size.

For years, I bought all of my shoes there for two reasons: One, I used to love to go to Tops and walk from room to room and look at everything they had to offer. And two, while the shoes were expensive, they had the only real selection of great-looking flats. And for any woman who loves to wear flats, you know how difficult they are to find.

Two things that I didn't like about shopping at Tops were the service and how difficult the actual buying process was. To go there and buy shoes was an investment of time. It took forever. They were always super busy and never had enough help. To try the shoes on, you needed a sales person to retrieve the right size from the stock room. So there was always a lot of waiting. Then after you found the shoes you wanted, you had to wait again in line at the register to actually purchase them.

So while the selection at Tops was amazing, the process of buying shoes was not easy. In addition, despite spending quite a bit of money there at least four times a year, no one at Tops knew my name, my shoe size or what style of shoe I liked. Each time I came into the store, I had to start all over giving my "shoe history."

9

Still, I shopped there and for the most part enjoyed it. I didn't really have a choice. They were the best store in town for quality flats. I really never gave it much thought until about three years ago when I heard some friends in my yoga class talking about Zappos, the online shoe retailer. My friends said that not only did Zappos deliver on their over-the-top selection of shoes, but they were legendary in the world of service. They understood how to make the shopping and buying process incredibly easy. That all sounded good to me, so I gave Zappos a shot.

And you know, I have been a Zappos customer every since. I have not gone back to Tops. Despite their direct-mail campaigns and beautiful window displays that I see every time I'm downtown. Why? Because from the first time I started shopping at Zappos, the experience has been exceptional. Rather than go downtown and spend hours in a shoe store, where despite spending hundreds of dollars no one knew my name or took an interest in me, I chose Zappos.

With Zappos, I can shop any time of the day or night that is convenient for me. I can buy and send back as many pairs of shoes as I like, no questions asked. They send me information on shoes they think I would like based on my "shoe history." And every single time I deal with Zappos, they seem genuinely excited I am buying shoes from them. I feel like I matter. (Make no mistake, this is not simply an Internet business vs. bricks-and-mortar retail story. There were plenty of companies selling shoes on-line before Zappos. This is a new-economy, customers-in-charge, pay-attention story.)

With Zappos entering the competitive landscape, Tops for Shoes' lack of customer service—that I used to accept as the way it was—now became my deciding factor (not price) on where to take my business. And that's a shift for Tops, for Zappos and for me, the customer.

The lesson here is that business owners who are still trying to do business according to the old rules will suffer the consequences, if they haven't already. Our products and services have become commodities. Consumers' choices on what to buy, where to buy it and when to buy it abound. The first rule in the Trust & Value Economy is that the customer is in control.

If business owners are still trying to compete in an economy where they believe they are in control—that the consumer needs their product or service, and needs them to sell it—they have missed or refused to accept that things have changed. Just having a quality product or superior service isn't enough anymore. In fact, my colleague Cindy Solomon of Cindy Solomon & Associates says that a quality product and superior service are just your "entry tickets" to the market these days.

And that's exactly where your opportunity in this new economy lies.

In this new economy, the economy doesn't matter

In 2006, Ray Jackson was enjoying life in Hawaii, selling luxury destination real estate that in all truth sold itself. When the economy began to shift in 2008, Ray, a 30-year veteran of the industry, watched in disbelief as this lucrative market evaporated. At the time, he had been, as were most professionals in destination real estate, at the top of his game. Selling and developing amazing properties. He had a backlog of buyers waiting in line to purchase pre-sells and condos that were mere drawings. Times were good—very good.

Then, almost out of nowhere came change, a serious change. As we all know, in 2008, the real estate bubble popped. At the same time, two local Hawaiian air carriers declared bankruptcy. Needless to say, the combined catastrophes wreaked havoc on the island's travel and tourism industry and were deadly to Ray's business. Ray watched helplessly as, overnight, buyers walked away and deals disappeared at the point of close, with no possible chance of returning and with no hope of seeing other buyers or deals take their places.

With no one left to sell to, Ray decided it was time to take a good long look at his career and determine if and how to move forward. So he critically examined all aspects of the real-estate business, his role in it and the economy in general. Through that analysis, he came to realize how little control he actually had or would ever have over the economy or for that matter over developers. To take charge of his own future, he decided he had to focus on what he could control and that is how he provides service to clients.

Surprising to some, Ray chose to return to luxury real estate and to do it in California, no less. But this time, he adhered to his new strategy. He dedicated himself to knowing who his clients are and finding out what they value. He dedicated himself to finding products/properties that matched their values—even if that meant passing a sale on to someone else. He built deep relationships and put the clients' needs ahead of sales goals. Not that he hadn't done some of that before in Hawaii. He had. But then, he did it more because it was his personality than because it was a part of his business plan. Now serving his customers was his principal mission. He was laser focused on their needs. He was selling with purpose.

All this meant he had to listen more, react less and engage at an entirely new level with his clients. Success in this economy means understanding clients at an intimate level, and then creating an experience that not only meets their needs but blows their minds. He quickly recognized that his ability to succeed was directly connected to his ability to connect, stand out and be memorable to his customers.

As of this writing, the real-estate market hasn't bounced back for the majority of the United States and certainly not in California. However, Ray is at the pinnacle of his career as vice-president of sales for Toscana Country Club in Indian Wells, California. Ray and his team just celebrated their third straight year of record sales. In fact, as this goes to publication, Ray is too busy to break away for a quick trip to his vacation home on the East Coast.

Imagine, selling real estate in this challenging economy and being too busy to break away. How many real-estate agents do you know in that position today?

So ask yourself, do you want to be successful in this new economy? Of course you do.

Begin by accepting that this is a new economy with new rules. And I don't care—and neither should you—what economists, experts and business gurus are saying or predicting. The truth is—no matter what the economy does—whether it goes up or goes down—on some level for you as a business owner it just doesn't matter. Yes, you heard me right, I said what the economy does just does not matter in terms of your ability to be successful.

Because no matter what the health of this economy is, the most important factor determining the success of your business in the Trust & Value Economy—as Ray discovered—is your customer. And that's great news.

Success in the Trust & Value Economy is far more about understanding your customer than about predicting market fluctuations. After all, if Ray can have record sales in luxury real estate in California post-2008, that's proof that there is opportunity in any field for anyone willing to do the work and embrace a new way of doing business.

By the way, Ray reports that he enjoys his job much more now than when he had clients lined up at the door. He feels real satisfaction in using his knowledge and expertise to help people find the right place to enjoy their lives.

Economy down—opportunity up

While as individuals we had no control over the events that caused the recession in the United States and around the globe, in its aftermath, there are opportunities for success in business that didn't exist under the previous system. And more opportunities are developing all the time.

To realize those opportunities, it is time to start looking at our businesses through a different set of eyes, not only as business owners but as consumers as well. So much has changed. Unlike other economies that are described as strong or weak, this one has shifted. And it is in that shift that you can find a bright future.

Economists agree that we are moving out of one economy and into another. They say we have moved out of a push economy and into a pull economy. And in a pull economy there is one very distinct difference: The consumers—not you, not the corporation, not the business owner—are in control. They are the ones making the decisions.

In strong economies, things are good, and we are all poised to invest and grow. Both the consumer and the business owner are confident. In weak economies, we all cut back and wait for things to get better.

However, in a shifting economy, the only thing we know for sure is that things are and will continue to be uncertain. This economy is different. We have never experienced anything like it. Thus, no one can be sure what is going to happen.

That uncertainty has created fear, mistrust and a lack of confidence in the market from the consumer. People are afraid to commit to too much. The result of months and years of this instability has actually changed the mindset of the consumer—how they think, what they want, what they value. We are living in different times. Not only has our economy changed, our society has changed as well.

But that doesn't mean the world has stopped. By no means. People still need goods and services. It's how they want them delivered and by whom that has changed. Understand that, learn what your customers want and find a way to meet their newly defined needs, and you'll be on you way to success in this new age.

In the Trust & Value Economy, it is not what we offer as professionals, but how we offer it that is truly our competitive advantage.

So with the right attitude, the right approach and some elbow grease, this can be your economy. Contrary to what the economic gurus are saying, this is a time of abundance, a time of unlimited choices, and a time to build and create a wealth of relationships and a wealth of opportunity. Welcome to the Trust & Value Economy, your path to success awaits you!

KEY TAKEAWAY

To win in the Trust & Value Economy, understand that the economy is not just down, it has changed and changed forever. Embracing this change is the first step to success in this economy.

CHAPTER 2

The Changing Landscape

If we look back over history, there are many examples of ideas and things that were commonplace in our culture that now seem odd or out of place. Things that were fixed and accepted at one time now have ceased to exist. The one thing you can count on from history is that nothing lasts forever. Things change.

To survive in this new economy, we should understand the scope of the change occurring and then be open to making the changes we need to succeed. Think about it: this is not the first time major changes have come to the world, and it certainly won't be the last.

The economy has evolved—and the successful will evolve with it

Let me put it in perspective. Let's go back to the age of the dinosaurs. Yes, I said the age of the dinosaurs. Who would have thought these giant creatures that dominated the Earth for millions of years could have been wiped out in a catastrophic event. Watching them go about, a spectator might have thought that these massive creatures were indestructible, a permanent part of the landscape and destined to rule the world for all time. But in the end, their size, strength, speed and prowess could not protect them—and may have even brought them down.

Their time of dominance eventually did come to an end. And with it came struggle and confusion for some species. Change and opportunity for others. Much like today's economic change.

The recent events that have sent shock waves through the global economy have served to end the reign of a number of corporate dinosaurs and severely cripple others. The days when a single massive corporation could dominate and devour smaller companies through sheer size and financial prowess are on their way to extinction. It is becoming increasingly apparent that the old way of doing business no longer works. Our long-standing business models, much like dinosaurs, are a dying breed.

This is not however cause for economic pessimism. In the same way that the dinosaur extinction gave rise to a new age of mammals, the recession and other economic changes have paved the way for a new time of abundance for those who will seize the moment and learn to thrive within its constructs.

Welcome to your new neighborhood—the global village

A huge part of this economic evolution is that you've gone global. We all have. Whether we own a multi-million dollar corporation or a consignment shop on Main Street, our marketplace today is the world. Our customer base, our suppliers and our competition know no boundaries.

We are more connected than ever. At the click of a button we can bid for the latest version of our favorite video game from a seller in Canada or London or India. We can hire vendors and consultants from anywhere in the world and work via Skype, video conference and online meetings.

But be aware, being global also means that we are no longer isolated from what goes on the rest of the world—good or bad. Whether you like that notion or not doesn't matter. It's a fact. And it's not going to change.

The events that occur in other parts of the world now influence our lives and our businesses. What happens in Brazil or Greece can have just as big an effect as what's happening in our local town.

> *I had dinner one night with a very successful owner of Honda dealerships in my town. He has owned and sold varying brands of automobiles over the years. About ten years ago, he decided to invest in Honda dealerships because he loved the cars and found them to be unbelievably reliable. A great product for his customers. As luck would have it, his customers loved the Hondas too. Every year, his business got better and better.*

> *Until March 2011, when a devastating tsunami hit Japan. That tragedy would not only severely cripple Japan's economy, but it also had major repercussions for dealerships around the world— including my friend's business. For the next two years, if you sold, worked on or drove a Japanese car, getting parts to fix or inventory to sell would prove to be nearly impossible. Auto dealers and mechanics in the United States had to wait for industry in Japan to come back before they were up and running again. And it is only recently that my friend's dealership has returned to normal.*

While the loss to dealerships obviously does not even come close to what the people of Japan suffered and continue to suffer from the tsunami, the story does demonstrate that we are more dependent on one another than we were even a generation ago. And as we move deeper into this new economy, that dependence is only likely to grow.

Now everyone is your customer...and your competition

For you and others willing to embrace the Trust & Value Economy, that growing dependence, growing connectedness, comes with great opportunity...and competition.

In the past, customers who were interested in buying most products or services were pretty much limited to dealing with businesses located close to where they lived. And consumers who lived in rural areas may have been limited to a single provider for their needs. As a result, business owners did not have to spend much time or investment to get above the "white noise" and consider whether they were building trust and offering consistent value to their customers. As business owners at that time, we focused more on building our business than pleasing our customer.

Today in our increasingly interconnected global village, buyers have more choices than ever before about where they are going to spend their money. The rising popularity of Internet businesses and the extensive shipping networks now available around the world have greatly expanded the marketplace for the consumer. Online shopping, toll-free order numbers, chat lines and the like mean that a customer does not need to be in the same city, state or even on the same continent to buy a product.

Like so many of you, I buy groceries for our home. Weekly I go to the grocery store and buy the milk, bread, etc. The one thing I don't buy weekly is coffee. Now I love coffee and I do buy it. But I buy it from Jamaica. Several years ago while working down there, I was served this wonderful coffee. And I loved it. I loved it so much I had some shipped home. When I ran out, I simply went to their website and purchased some more. In fact, all I had to do was mark that I wanted my order to be recurring and direct-billed to my credit card. So now I not only buy my everyday coffee in Jamaica, I do so with ease. In fact, due to the online capabilities in this economy, it is actually less of a hassle to buy my coffee from Jamaica than to get it from just down the street.

Ten years ago, I would have had to wait for my next trip to Jamaica. Or I would have had to call the shop, go through a long process and paid a prohibitive price because it's not likely they would have been set up for long-distance shipping. In the Trust & Value Economy, I have the luxury of buying what I want with ease no matter where it is in the world.

Now, you have to admit this takes competition to a whole new level and expands the definition. The globalization of the market makes staying competitive more demanding. You must stay aware of trends from competitors well beyond the radius of the traditional geographical limits within which you would expect your clients to purchase.

However, as challenging as this makes competition, there is an upside, a big upside. It gives you the same opportunity my Jamaican coffee dealer has. It allows you to reach out to potential customers you would never have even thought of as prospects 20 years ago. It gives you the opportunity to work with a bigger market and have the chance to build a clientele far larger than you could have ever imagined in a localized economy. This economy may have broadened your scope of competition, but it has also greatly expanded your customer base.

Technological advancements have revolutionized how we do business. On the one hand, they have levelled the playing field and given small businesses the best shot they have ever had at competing with the big boys, those corporate giants. On the other hand, technology has added an entire new area—a new landscape—to which you, the business owner, must adapt.

Step into a new age

The marketplace has changed irrevocably and businesses, corporations and professionals must evolve right along with it to remain competitive. The tried and true business principles that dominated the US economy for so many years have lost their relevance in this global landscape. To survive in this economy, you must understand the scope of the changes occurring and then be open to making the changes you need to make—changes that will impact your business, your customer and your world.

For the savvy businessperson who takes the time to learn the ins and outs of the changing economic climate, these new developments can be major advantages. The very same shifts that spell disaster for businesses and corporations stuck in their old ways present a world of opportunity for businesses and professionals that know how to capitalize on them.

You already know that the age-old methods in business practice are no longer viable. The dinosaurs are all but extinct. The age of start-up companies and community business partnering has begun.

The most important step on the road to turning this moment of opportunity into a lifetime of success is to learn about and appreciate who your customers are and how you reach them—and reach them more resolutely than ever before. Are you ready to step up and embrace the chance to make this new economic landscape a landscape of abundance for your business?

You will have to be open and dramatically shift the ways you think about business, networking, long-term success and the global market. In the following chapters, you will discover the mindset and techniques you will need to adopt in order to engage and truly connect with customers in this new economy and achieve the success you are seeking. The opportunity is already there waiting. Let's begin the journey and embrace the chance to make this new economy your time of achievement.

KEY TAKEAWAY

To win in The Trust & Value Economy understand that the business landscape has changed; you work in a global village with no boundaries, no borders.

CHAPTER 3

The Changed Consumer

So, we're agreed. The economy has shifted. And technology has radically redefined the way we do business. However, the most important and fundamental shift in this economy to be aware of— the one your success in the Trust & Value Economy will be built on—is the shift in the consumer mindset.

Consumers have been through the wringer

When the economy started to struggle in late 2008, so did the consumer—emotionally as well as financially. At first, consumers, like businesses, contentedly waited for the economy to bounce back. It always had before. But when the first bounce took longer and was far less impressive than expected, consumer confidence began to wane. With each consecutive bounce up and then right back down, any faith that was left in our economy and in any institution's ability to fix it became exhausted.

With the very real chance that their personal cash supply could be cut off at any time from job loss, loss in home equity or loss of investment income, consumers started slashing their household budgets and paying down their credit cards. The new boat, the new car, the vacation would have to wait. With the state of the economy so completely out of the individual's control, people sought ways to assume some control over their financial security. They decided to hold onto their money, unless they had a very good reason to spend it All of a sudden, it was more of a status symbol to save than to spend. And the idea of being debt free sounded smarter and smarter.

And who can blame them for pulling back, for becoming cautious with their money? They have had a rough go of it. With the economic downturn, many businesses simply turned their backs on their customers. In the last few years, consumers have found themselves saddled with homes in developments that never built the promised pool and golf course. They have invested in small banks that went under. They have put their money in big companies that sold them out when they took bailouts or sold to other companies. They have watched as their own retirements and 401(k)s have dropped due to bad decisions made by corporations—decisions in which the consumer had no input. And on and on the stories go. When you think about it that way; it's amazing we get anyone to buy anything these days

In the Trust & Value Economy, trust is not going to come easy with your customers. Research study after research study is showing that the spending habits of consumers have greatly changed since 2008. This economy is uncertain. The constant fluctuations have created a more cautious consumer. Consumers are thinking longer and more carefully about every purchase they make.

So today when consumers do want to buy—and they do want to buy—they also want to be sure about what they are investing in and with whom they are investing. It is not the product or service that consumers are searching for these days; it is the opportunity to find and work with professionals they can trust and those who value them as customers.

Now they're in charge

And heaven help the company that doesn't live up to those demands. While customers today are more cautious, less trusting, and more selective about where and with whom they are going to do business— they are also in charge and they know it.

Globalization, advancement in technology and increased competition have put the consumer in the driver's seat when they set out to make a purchase. They can buy directly from an online retailer or go to a bidding site. They can find an independent producer who has put a homemade spin on a product or find a used version at a markdown. And even when they are inside an actual store, they can use their smart phones to get reviews on a product and check prices. Some studies say as many as 90 percent of us "Google" before we ever call, visit or engage with a business.

But really, what are consumers looking for spending so much time gathering information?

Remember, consumers today are skittish. They have been burned. So they want to make sure they are getting the best value for their money. They want to learn something about the company's products, values and service standards before they open their wallets. Consumers who are willing to spend money and willing to pay more will only do so if they believe that what they are buying is worthy of their investment. They are looking for Trust & Value.

And there is no shortage of websites out there to help them educate themselves. With the click of a mouse, consumers can check out product reviews and service ratings. Bloggers are not shy about writing positive or scathing reviews on companies. Social media outlets have taken the most powerful form of advertising—word-of-mouth—to a whole new level. And your current customers can share a positive or negative experience with people they know at lightning speed.

In fact, I was on Facebook one night and saw a young mother post that she was looking for a pediatric dentist. There were several responses, but the one that caught my eye was harsh and negative about a dentist in our town. The commenter shared how this dentist, whom she named, was not only a bad dentist but was also rude and cruel to her children.

Now, not only did the young mother who was asking the question see that comment but so did everyone else she had "friended" on Facebook. Anyone following that thread anywhere around the world could see that post and the name of that dentist boldly and clearly. This is not exactly the type of review you as a business owner or professional would like to read. Other Internet users will read the information and make a decision about that dentist and move on. They most likely will not stop to consider that there may be another side to the story.

But it's not only the small business that is affected by word-of-mouth these days. The Internet has given consumers the power to bring down huge corporations.

Remember hearing about musician David Carroll and United Airlines? David's guitar was broken while in the care of the airline's baggage handlers. But the story gets worse. He reported the incident immediately after it occurred. According to David's account, at least three United employees showed complete indifference towards him and his plight. So his next step was to file an official claim with the airline. Their response? They said he was ineligible for compensation because he had failed to make the claim within the company's stipulated standard 24-hour timeframe—something each of the three employees he had dealt with earlier failed to tell him.

He tried for more than nine months to get the situation fixed. He had no luck. No one cared or listened.

In the old days, David would have been feeling pretty helpless after nine months. He may have told a few friends about how awful he and his guitar had been treated. But in today's world, he wrote a song about it, created a simple music video and posted it on YouTube.

In one day, more than 150,000 people saw the video. Within six months, the video and what it had to say about United Airlines had more than 10 million views. And David wound up on all the major news channels telling his story. You can imagine what that failure of customer service ended up costing United Airlines. A lot more than one Taylor Guitar. Now that's power.

Don't be disheartened. The upside of this consumer power for business owners is that providing a "wow" customer experience can result in a review that drives people to your door. When a satisfied customer with a large social media following posts a status update complete with pictures about an amazing latte they just got at a coffee shop, dozens, maybe hundreds, of other consumers may feel compelled to try it and pass their experience on to their "friends." And that kind of advertising you cannot buy.

But whether positive or negative, what's important is that the ball is clearly in the consumers' court and the options of where to buy and from whom are endless.

And that's where you can add real value and gain a competitive advantage.

Consumers still need your guidance

While all this choice might seems great, in reality it can be debilitating for consumers. Technology has advanced, but our human capacity to process and filter information has not improved enough to match the flood of choices inherent in today's buying decisions.

In his book, *The Paradox of Choice*, Barry Schwartz cautions that giving consumers more product choices lowers their purchase satisfaction. You read that right—more choices equals lower gratification. He surmises that a vast array of choices leaves us feeling like we missed out, resulting in anxiety, stalled decision-making and even regret after purchase.

Adding to that, a survey of more than 7,000 worldwide consumers cited in the May 2012 *Harvard Business Review* shows that choices can actually breed discontent. The study found that consumers spend much more time researching products today compared with the past and yet 70 percent don't decide definitively which brand to buy until the point of purchase. They narrow their choice, but they do not make a final decision until they experience the business, see the product and interact with the business. Ironically, post-purchase, one-fifth of consumers actually continue to research the product to affirm their choice. And 40 percent of consumers report feeling anxious about their decision after they've completed the transaction.[1] (Meaning service after the sale has become critical to maintaining your customer base.)

As a business owner in the Trust & Value Economy, this information is invaluable. Your job from this day forward is to help your customers find their way through the clutter and make that buying decision easy. Remember, today consumers are not looking for a product or service, they are looking for someone they can trust to provide them with value for their dollar.

To get started, ask yourself these four questions:

1. **How has your specific customer changed in this new economy?**
   Step back and think about your customers. Get clear about the problems or changes they may be facing, and what, if any, opportunities you see in those challenges.

2. **How does your product or service fit their new reality?**
   Once you understand your customers' most pressing challenges, ask yourself what your product or service does to help. Get clear on how your product or service can solve their problems or help them take advantage of opportunities.

3. **What kind of value are you offering them?**
   What is your customer getting from you that goes above and beyond? Think about the "little extras" you provide that make customers feel important or special.

4. **What makes you stand out from the competition?**
   Again, what you are selling is a commodity. Your customers can

---

1 http://hbr.org/product/Harvard-business-review-may-2012/an/BR1205-MAG-Eng

buy your product from anyone, anywhere, at anytime. Know exactly why they should buy it from you

The answers to these questions will put you on the path to being able to truly be of service to your customers and thus on the path to winning in the Trust & Value. Economy. If you make their lives easier, their challenges less, their worries lower, consumers will choose to buy from you. Who wouldn't choose a business that could do that?

The challenge here is that trust and value cannot be traditionally sold. They have to be built. And don't forget that while technology presents our consumers with unlimited choices, it also gives us business owners incredible capabilities to touch our consumers in ways that can help us start the process of building trust and value. We can now easily capture and manage relevant information, so we can engage with customers in meaningful ways and establish mutually beneficial relationships. (We'll get into just exactly how to do that in later chapters.)

Today's consumer requires a new level of connection, engagement and relationship. Success in the Trust & Value Economy depends on your ability to build and invest in that relationship. And that's a very rewarding way to do business.

KEY TAKEAWAY

To win in the Trust & Value Economy, be aware that your customers today are cautious, well-informed and empowered—and they know it.

CHAPTER 4

Embrace Change; Revel In Opportunity

L et's just say it out loud: We hate change.

Most people do. If we have a choice, most of us prefer to get into a comfortable routine for our activities– including how we run our businesses—and stick with it. Yet, while the idea of "if it ain't broke, don't fix it" may seem like the safest and easiest philosophy, it's actually one way to guarantee that your business will not survive, especially in this economy. (Then you'll really be pushed out of your comfort zone.)

The Trust & Value Economy is all about getting comfortable with uncertainty and inconsistency. It is an economy of unpredictability. So achieving success these days means getting comfortable with change, being flexible and adaptive. This is not an economy or a consumer you can predict.

Too often professionals and business owners fear and thus avoid change. They choose to wall themselves off from the world and hide in their routine. They hope that if they just keep plugging along, doing what they've always done, they'll get by.

But that's not the way it works in life or in business in the 21st century.

Don't change if you don't want to…to succeed, that is

Change is going to happen. And in the Trust & Value Economy, it's going to happen a lot more than it used to. You do, however, have a choice on how you react to that change. There, feel like you have some control?

One option is to adopt a siege mentality in which you decide to take cover until the perceived threat (change) has passed. While that certainly is a choice, adopting this mentality unfortunately will provide with you a false sense of security.

It is sort of like retreating to a castle when the advancing army is hot on your heels. Unless the castle possesses massive reserves of food and water, and a bigger army inside, you really have no chance of avoiding your impending fate. You may be able to keep the advancing army at bay for a little while, but ultimately they will catch up with you.

The same is true for your business. You can try to avoid change, but you can't stop the world around you from changing. As long as you continue to idealize the past as "the way we always did it," and try to operate your business as if nothing has changed, you are robbing yourself of the opportunity to capitalize on the positive changes that present chances for your company to grow and prosper

So your other option in dealing with change is to face it head on. The truth is that if you are open to change and reach out to meet it when you see it coming toward you, change can provide all the momentum you need to flourish.

It's a funny fact about us as human beings, even when we are uncomfortable and unhappy in our current state, we avoid changing it. How does the saying go? We'd rather stay with the certainty of an unhappy future than risk the possibility of happiness in the unknown. That is how rooted we are in status quo, and how much we prefer predictability to risk.

The irony is that sticking to the tried and true, at least in the Trust & Value Economy, can be one of the greatest risks you as a business owner could ever take. Staying with the status quo in this economy will ensure constant struggle, if not total extinction.

You're already good at change

Honestly, you might not like change, but you are already are a master of it. If you think about it, you have been dealing successfully with change all of your life. Are you the same person you were when you were 16 or even 21? No, you are not. In fact, you are far from it.

And thank goodness. Other than having smooth skin and smaller hips, there isn't too much I miss about being either 16 or 21. I am grateful for the changes I have had to make in my life; changes that have helped me grow into the person I am.

And I'd be willing to bet that if you take a good look in the mirror, you will have admit that you have changed quite a bit too over the years—and you are happy about it. You've changed schools, changed jobs, changed your mind, changed your style, changed your priorities, maybe even changed your worldview. And with every change, you've grown, gained wisdom, learned to handle life's curve balls and become a better person—adding value all along the way.

Well, what's true for you is true for your business.

The world is going to keep changing all around us. That's a given.

And whether or not we want them to, those changes will affect our businesses. If we want to survive, we need to recognize the change for whatever it is and decide how best to adapt for our clients and for ourselves.

Exit the comfort zone; enter success

So change is not something to be feared; it is something to be embraced. After all, it is where your opportunity lies.

For most of us, the root cause of our discomfort with change is fear. The most challenging thing about this new economy is that no one can accurately predict what is going to happen. And without accurate predictions, we think we lack the ability to plan, to design a step-by-step process to success, to do the things that make us feel safe and in control.

Now don't panic. I am not implying that just because the economy is chaotic that your business plan should be too. Quite the opposite. I'm suggesting you accept change as inevitable and plan accordingly. Research consequences. Make educated choices. Take calculated risks to overcome new challenges and take advantage of new opportunities.

Think about the people we know who do the most dangerous types of work. Firefighters. Police officers. High-rise construction workers. Racecar drivers. They aren't usually complete daredevils who thumb their noses at peril. They understand that their workplace is full of uncertainty and unpredictability. They understand and appreciate the potential for serious injury or death. But rather than allowing themselves to be paralyzed by fear, they take appropriate steps to lower the risk of something unfortunate happening. Better yet, they take appropriate steps to heighten the chance of getting a better than expected result.

Though they cannot eliminate the potential for negative outcomes in their professions, they can learn from the experiences of others and adopt the best possible practices to ensure the safety of their entire team. Their acceptance of uncertainty and risk also leads to opportunities, and ways for their organizations and their people to develop what, without embracing change, they would never have uncovered.

In the Trust & Value Economy, we need to learn from those who embrace uncertainty every day. Keep in mind, there is no need to be flying blind in the face of change.

- Be proactive and be prepared

- Remain aware of happenings in the market

- Research the experiences of others who have adopted the practices you are considering for your business; this will let you see how those changes performed

- Move at a manageable pace. Choose to make small changes with limited potential to impact the overall success of your business, rather than a sweeping overhaul that could make or break your entire future.

Taking these actions can allow you to move forward in shifting markets without throwing your company into chaos or worrying about the future. Calculated risk can make even those most fearful among us more comfortable with the process.

Being proactive, being ready for change, keeps you ready to jump on opportunity, minimize challenges long before they become major threats, and flex when the market demands.

While you can't control everything that happens in your organization, you have absolute control over how you see change and how you respond to it. You alone can choose to walk toward change with your arms outstretched to embrace it or to hunker down and hope you have sufficient resources to wait out a change that may prove to be permanent. Your choice will depend largely on whether you see change as a tool that can help you and your business grow or as a threat to the comfortable old methods you know. Seeing change as a purely negative will only rob you of opportunity.

Take change for a ride

The best way to take advantage of change is to get ahead of it. And ahead of it is where you want to be to win in the Trust & Value Economy.

To get ahead, take your head out of the day-to-day grind and examine what is going on in the rest of the world, in the market, in your field. These days, what happens external to your operations has just as much, if not more, impact than your internal business decisions.

I recommend that my clients take a breather at least every other month and set aside some time with their team and/or outside advisors to take a closer look at changing trends, world events and anything external that may have an impact on their customers or services. There's nothing like a big brainstorming session to discuss what is going on with customers, in society, politically, and in the industry at large, to shift your thinking and put you on a path to ensure you stay ahead of the curve. Being open to new ideas and thinking outside of your business will ensure you are the one driving change instead of letting it drive you.

I have a client who runs a fairly large architectural firm in Atlanta, Georgia. I work with his high potentials and next-level leadership, both as a group and on an individual coaching level. This effort of remaining aware of market changes external to the firm is a major part of what we work on.

Three months into this project, we held our first session. What we discovered, among other things, was that two major competitors were going through some pretty radical changes themselves. One was disbanding, and several partners were either retiring or leaving to join other firms. The other firm was merging with a much larger company based out of California. Both of these changes had the potential to make a tremendous impact on our business development initiatives.

The firm I was working with had not been focused on the clients of these two other firms because they felt many of their clients were long-term and loyal. But now they saw a major opportunity. They knew the window would be short. So they immediately realigned their business development strategy to focus heavily on these new opportunities in the market.

The result—25 percent growth rate over last year's business development goals. I think you would agree that this is strong growth for a company hoping just to remain flat in terms of growth in a shifting economy.

Change and change often

I would both argue and caution you that if you are not redefining and adjusting your strategies and actions at least two to three times a year, you probably aren't paying enough attention. This economy is moving fast, and you need to move with it. In fact, you need to move ahead of it.

The Trust & Value Economy provides the perfect environment for you to continue to bend and shape your plan according to changing needs. Even the strategic or annual plan you've established needs to be revisited and adjusted as outside events and situations—largely your customers' needs—dictate. Don't get caught in the trap of believing that once finished, strategic plans are complete. In today's economy, designing the strategy is just the beginning. (More on this in Chapter 7.)

Learning to sift through changes to find the positive possibilities will put you and your company in a position to grow and adapt no matter what the fluctuating global economy brings your way.

KEY TAKEAWAY

To win in the Trust & Value Economy, embrace change as the opportunity to take your business to new heights. Make change part of your business strategy.

CHAPTER 5

It's About Trust & Value—Not Price

A few years ago, I was working at a conference in Dallas, Texas. The room was full of about 400 dentists, with the average dentist in that room grossing about $600,000 a year. Now that is a substantial gross for a dentist. Most gross is around $400,000 or $450,000. So, lucky me, I was working with a group of high-performing dentists.

However, two of the dentists in that room grossed more than $1 million a year. Both were from small and very rural communities. In fact, one dentist came from a town with a population of less than 50,000. In addition, both million-dollar dentists offered the same services as the other dentists in that room. So you have to wonder, don't you? Why were these two dentists able to produce so much more revenue than the average dentist in the United State and more than the high-performing dentists in that room?

The answer is simple; they knew how to sell trust and value, and they focused on these instead of on selling price.

People buy what they value—regardless of price

Hard truth: If your customers leave you over price, it is because price was all you were selling. And there's no profit in price. People choose price when there is no other option—and that's especially true in the Trust & Value Economy.

Think about your own buying behavior. Think about the American public. Why do people buy organic produce, pay for an upgrade on an airplane, or pay for water in a bottle? All of those products are more expensive than their unqualified counterparts—regular produce, tourist class and tap water. People pay more because they perceive value. They believe there is something there worth paying for. The sales professional or organization has done a great job of helping the buyer understand what that value is and how it benefits them. Buyers know they can get a similar product for less, but they would rather pay more and get the value that's meaningful to them. We buy what we feel is important for us to have, what we perceive brings value and benefit to our lives.

Sell from a place of value

So, as a sales professional, let me ask you, when you are talking to a prospect, do you lead with price? Of course not! (If you do, you are order taking not selling.)

You know focusing on cost at the start of your conversation can derail the entire sales process. So why, if you clearly would never begin a sales conversation there, do you derail the conversation by defaulting to price later? Why? The truth is that most of us were taught to sell from a place of weakness rather than a place of power.

Too many sales leaders have created environments where the reward is for selling quantity not quality.

Now I have told you over and over that the consumers are in control in this economy, and they know it. But that does not mean that as the business owner or sales professional you are down and out and weak. Far from it. It means you need to adjust and find where your opportunity is in this economy. And as we've discussed, it's not in price. Remember your product or service is but a mere commodity in this market.

Selling quantity over quality might have worked in an economy when competition was slim, margins were fat, and the business was controlling the buying cycle. But in the Trust & Value Economy, there is no room for a portfolio full of customers who are not willing to meet your price and pay a fair value for your product or service. To win in this economy, you need to focus on prospects and customers who understand and appreciate the value of the relationship they have with you and your company and are willing to pay for it. To attract and retain those types of customers, your focus needs to be on building trust and adding value first, with price coming in much, much later.

I worked with an engineering firm whose goal was to work less and make more. Great goal, right! The first thing we did was look at their portfolio to review where they were competing and winning solely on price. In other words, we determined what clients they had that truly were not earning them profit, and therefore not really adding any value.

We then eliminated more than 20 percent of their client base. Imagine that, in a shifting economy, just eliminating 20 percent of your customer base. The result? At the end of the year, their profits grew by more than 10 percent. In fact, they had never had profit percentages that high. Why? For the first time, they stopped competing on price and started competing on value. They quit selling from a place of weakness and began selling from a place of power.

Make price a detail

In the Trust & Value Economy, your goal should always be to demonstrate how your product or service will make an impact, solve a problem, enhance the product, or give your customer peace of mind.

You did not get into the business you're in because you are passionate about low pricing (unless you're Sam Walton). You had an idea or concept you believed would help someone get what they wanted, or you wanted to take on the challenge of delivering a service in a new and better way. That is a big part of the value you offer. Once your customer is able to see and appreciate that value, the price becomes secondary and certainly not a deal breaker. This strategy hinges on your ability to build trust with your prospect long before you are in a position to offer them a solution to their problem, as well as your ability to deeply communicate and relate the value of your product or service.

When we talk about customers and the strategy of growing your company or meeting your goals we use the words "buy" and "sell". We do so because they speak to the core transaction of business. But buying and selling are so much more than the definitions we give them in our culture and our society, and especially in this economy.

As you think about those terms as they relate to the Trust &

Value Economy, I would like you to see buying as recognizing value, selecting who to reward with the fruits of our labor. It is some of the most scrutinized decision-making we engage in as human beings.

Selling is putting yourself and your reputation on the line behind a product or service you believe in. Seriously serving your customers is vastly different than just making them believe you have what they need. When you focus on how to make your customers' lives better by providing value, you don't have to "sell" them on your product. They engage and want to buy it. And once customers decide they want your product, then price becomes merely a detail.

Trust before value. Value before price

Timing is also important. Build trust before value. Build value before price. The earlier price is discussed in your interactions, the more likely your customers are to focus on the expense, not the value of having a problem solved.

If customers ask early on about price, validate their question. Then, be honest that you cannot discuss price until you fully understand what they need and how you can help. Do that because it is true. All too often we undersell or oversell a prospect or customer, because we did not take the time to uncover the depth of their need. To truly service customers and help them ensure they are comparing apples to apples (when comparing your product to that of your competitor) put value on the table before you discuss dollars. Otherwise, it can seem as if so it you are giving a number and then trying to justify it.

People genuinely believe that they get what they pay for. So if your customers trusts you, if you have invested the time to identify their issues, and if you have fully explained the solution you can provide, then pricing that reflects the value that your product will give them should be welcomed by them. Why? Because the prospects understand their return on investment. In other words, they understand what is in it for them.

Selling in this style ensures that there will be a ready market for your services—no matter where your price point happens to be. You've spent money, assumed risk and put forth significant effort to be in a position to help to your customer in the first place. You should not feel wrong about asking a fair value for your contribution to the marketplace. In this case, what they pay for includes the most important services you offer—trust and value.

To gain a true competitive advantage over your competition, to enjoy the selling process and most importantly to truly serve your customers and prospects, do not compete on price. This is not the way to build your business in the Trust & Value Economy.

Instead, keep a laser focus on your customers and what you can do for them. Cater to their values. Engage them. Commit to establishing trust through long-term business relationships with them. Establish a reputation for excellence within your target market by providing products and service that your customers can count on for high quality and consistency.

Creating an environment that fosters customer loyalty and continued value must be an on-going exercise. Building trust and loyalty with your customer base is a continual journey for your business, not a destination. Dan Allison, CEO of Vitalize Consulting Solutions (VCS), a technology services firm based in Boston, believes so much in the importance of standing out on value rather than price that he has built it into VCS's business model.

In the world of technology services, competition is heavy to say the least. Dan and his team of professionals face multiple competitors for every job they go after. And even after they land the job and begin working with the client, the competition keeps coming, trying to steal the business away.

"We have to be on our toes, providing a quality product in a timely manner is just not enough. Our market is price-sensitive to say the least, but given what we do and who we work with, providing a fantastic product at a good price is barely enough to open the door and certainly will not ensure we win the business or keep it," Dan says.

In order to gain a competitive advantage and create opportunity in the market, Dan knew his company would need to offer something unique and different. His firm looked at the market, reviewed their competitors and designed a value-added strategy. They deeply understand who their competitors are, what they offer, and what the competitors' business models and products are offering and delivering to the marketplace. They also deeply understand who their customers are, and more importantly, who their customers are not. They know their customers' value point—what their customers truly want, need and deem important beyond a quality product and a fair price. In other words, VCS knows beyond the basics what "value-addeds" make their target customer want to choose to work with one competitor over another.

With that information in place, Dan designed VCS's value-added strategy that makes winning and retaining business a much greater possibility for the sales professionals and the company. "We understand who we are, what we are about, and what we offer our customers over our competition," explains Dan. "To be *successful in this economy, it takes strong company identification and commitment to what you are offering and providing to your client above and beyond. You need to be able to articulate that, not only at the senior level but throughout your company." He adds, "If every person who works for you cannot articulate your value-added strategy, then what hope do you have that your customers understand and value why they are doing business with you? And if your customers do not firmly understand why they chose you over your competitors, chances are they won't be working with you for very long."*

Trust & Value take time

Since what you are truly selling is Trust & Value, you need to accept that it will take some time to win the confidence of your prospect in order to make him or her feel comfortable about making a purchase. Trust takes time to develop, period. People are naturally cautious about accepting information being presented to them by someone they don't know very well. This is especially true in the modern business climate where marketing campaigns frequently cross the fine line between crafting an appealing public image for a product and blatantly false advertising. Respect and trust are, therefore, precious commodities, well worth taking the time to cultivate in business relationships.

Once a prospect trusts that you are presenting yourself and your company in a fair and accurate manner, and that you are more interested in helping them get what they need than helping yourself, getting them to take the next step and buy from you is a much easier process—for both of you.

The more often a prospect interacts with you and your staff, the more invested they become in maintaining a positive relationship with your company. When the time comes to decide where to buy necessary products, the customer is going to choose to do business with a company that is already familiar to them, one they feel connected to. Since most purchasing decisions (initiated by a customer or prospect) are made to meet an immediate need, starting the process of establishing a relationship and developing trust with a provider is usually neither practical nor possible at that point.

If you have already taken the steps required to build trust and demonstrated that you can provide value with your product line, you have created a scenario in which it will be very difficult for your competition to even get a seat at the table.

What goes around comes around—big time

In the Trust & Value Economy, sales is a lifestyle, not a task that we do. As sales professionals, helping people is the way we live. We need to be always listening, always helping others find solutions, and always putting the needs of our prospects and clients above our own. When we sell this way, sales takes on a life of its own, and price becomes far less of an issue as our clients choose us, our advocates refer us business, and we gain confidence from selling from a position of power rather than of need. We need to be building relationships with prospects and customers long before they have a need. Purchasing decisions made to meet future needs or opportunities are the true goal of the sales professional looking to win in the Trust & Value Economy. Adding trust and value goes to a whole new level when your customers look to you to help them discover their buying needs.

To gain a true advantage over your competition, don't get bogged down in price gouging wars with other similar companies. This is not the way to build your business in the Trust & Value Economy. Stand out from the competition by adopting an entirely different business strategy that allows you to keep your focus firmly fixed on your customers and what you can do for them. By creating an atmosphere of trust and partnership with all prospective buyers (whether they become buyers or not), you will ensure that your company is the first choice that comes to their mind when the time comes to make serious purchases.

So good-bye cold calling. And hello trust building.

KEY TAKEAWAY

To win in the Trust & Value Economy, sell from a place of power. Build trust, add value and focus on your client's return on investment.

CHAPTER 6

You Are Now the CEO Of Customer Service

So you think you already provide great customer service? Well, it's like the title of Marshall Goldsmith's book says, "What Got You

Here Won't Get You There." Customer service in the Trust & Value Economy needs to be "super-sized." If ever there were a time when a business could get away with offering a good product without caring about customer satisfaction, that time is long gone.

In today's economy, how well you engage and treat the customer matters. It is the path to profitability.

I love that about the Trust & Value Economy. Sales professionals and business owners who don't prioritize, role model and exhibit the highest customer service standards are going to struggle, and probably cease to exist. In this economy, your customer service program needs to be front and center in your business. And your expectations around what it delivers need to expand.

Customers make the rules—Period

A couple of years ago my husband I found ourselves with a week off in August and no vacation plans. He had forgotten he had blocked the time, and told his staff to schedule their vacations. With their plans firmly in place, we knew we had to do something. Luckily I had nothing pending or booked on my calendar, I love to travel, so I jumped at the chance to plan this vacation. My husband, Rob, left it all up to me!

I suggested we head to Bar Harbor, Maine. You see Rob had never been there, and I had spent summers there as a child and just loved it. Rob thought it sounded great, so I booked our flight, our hotel room, made the executive decision to leave the rest of the vacation up in the air. As we lead such scheduled lives, thought it would be fun to just play it by ear, and see what comes up. I thought we'd figure it out when we got there.

Bar Harbor was everything I remembered; the town was quaint, the food was amazing, and the opportunities for outdoor fun, our favorite kind, were endless. We hiked, we rode mountain bikes, we fished, and we ate more blueberry ice cream than any two people ought to eat. The entire trip was more than we expected. The community was welcoming, the people were so nice, and even for a tourist town they went above and beyond to welcome us there.

From the time we stepped off the plane in Bangor to the time we headed home, I would describe us, for the most part, as quite satisfied customers. Everyone we encountered met our expectations, and so did the activities from the hiking to mountain biking, and the fabulous food. However there is one person, one company and one event that really stands out. Really stands head and shoulders above all other people and activities. One that made this trip memorable, worth talking about, and yes, exceeded expectations.

You see, I had just one request when we decided to vacation in Bar Harbor, one thing I wanted to do when we got there, and one thing my parents never seemed to let me do. When we vacationed there when I was a child, I always had this one request of my parents, yet no matter how much I begged, cried, pleaded they never let me do it. The request was simple, I always wanted to go out on the water. That is it, and I didn't care whether it was in a canoe , a raft, it just didn't matter. I just wanted to go out on some non-motorized contraption to view the scenery, the wildlife and just see Maine from the water.

So as soon as we arrived, as soon as Rob and I got settled in at the hotel, we immediately asked about doing just that. Going on a canoe trip or a sea kayaking tour. The concierge at the hotel recommended we go to a place called Coastal Adventures, a guide and adventure activity store just up the street. Now, among one of the many things I love about Bar Harbor, Maine, is that you can walk or bike anywhere and at any time. So out the door we went, and we walked up to Coastal Adventures to find out about our options and hopefully sign up for our trip. The moment we stepped into the Coastal Adventures shop, the amazing experience began. Our first encounter was with a lovely woman named Sue. She walked out from behind the counter, with a big smile on her face, and she welcomed us into the place. Sue immediately asked where we were from, what brought us to Bar Harbor. She was interested in hearing about everything we'd done since we had arrived in town. Then she wanted to know how she could help, what it was we needed.

I felt so comfortable, so at ease, that I found myself telling her my story. I went on to tell her that I had come to Bar Harbor as a child, and while I loved it, I had never gotten to do the one thing I had always wanted to do and that was go out on the water. I even laughingly told her it was because my horrid parents would not let me. She laughed along and said that she had just the trip for us. She said we needed to get signed up for the sunset kayaking tour. She went on to share that the scenery is incredible and the wildlife is at its best at that time of night. As she talked about the trip, she was so descriptive, she painted this picture that just sounded amazing, so of course we were in. Not one to miss a detail, Sue also made sure to ask what we wanted, what was most important to us, and what specifically they could do to make the trip special. Asking why specifically I had always wanted to do this.

I told her that I really didn't know, but I guess if I thought about it, there is something just so peaceful about the water, so calming.

The water, for me, just always seemed to be the best place where I could view and learn about the wildlife, and about the plants, and the history of Bar Harbor. Sue's eyes and nodding head told me she was listening, and smiled and then added that she would sign us up to go on a trip with Tom, one of their more experienced guides. Sue went on to explain that Tom was not only an experienced and well-trained guide, he was also the guide that had the most passion for this area. "He knows it like the back of his hand," she added, "and he will share stories with you, tell you the history of Bar Harbor, and most importantly you can ask him anything you want to and he will most likely know, or believe that he will make it his mission to find out!" She then attended to one last detail. She looked at the weather forecast and said "Wednesday night looks like the best night," and asked if could we would be available to go then? With no schedule on our part, no plans, we said absolutely yes.

So Wednesday night we took the stroll from our hotel up to Coastal Adventures, to go on our trip, the trip I had always wanted to take. So, as you can imagine, my expectations were high. Some more nice people who worked at the shop helped us get fitted out in our equipment, find our van and get us all set and ready to go. Before we knew it, we were sitting on the van, among the other kayakers, ready for the adventure of a lifetime, when on to our van walks this gregarious young guy, and I just knew it, from the moment I saw him, that this was our guide, Tom. When he first stepped on to the van, the energy level changed — it went up and his smile was just full of fun.

Sure enough, I was right. It was Tom. He introduced himself to us, one-by-one, shaking our hands, repeating our names and thanking us each for coming. As the van pulled away and started down the road, he took a seat in the center of the van, where everyone could see and hear him. He again thanked us for being there and asked each of us to share with the group what brought us on board, why we chose this tour. Slowly we started sharing our answers, and Tom very skillfully wove all of our comments into a conversation about the trip, about our surroundings, and about the history of Bar Harbor. Without any of us realizing what he had done, Tom had answered our questions, told us the details of the trip, and had us laughing as he added to it and punched it all up with stories. What started as a van full of strangers, now just felt like twelve friends with whom we had decided to go on a sea kayaking adventure.

Before any of us even realized it, we had traveled the forty-five minutes to the other side of the island, and we were ready to head off on this adventure. Tom, being a guide after all, went over the safety tips, and again shared what we would be doing. He did his last safety check, just to make sure we had everything in place and everything secure. Then we were off!

The entire sea kayaking tour was incredible, it was so beautiful, and we thought Sue could not have been more right. The sunset sea kayaking tour was just the right choice, and on this night it was spectacular. We were having a great time—no an amazing time—and Tom was a big reason why. Tom kept the group together, he kayaked with us and talked with each of us and got us talking with one another. His knowledge of the area was superb. The trip was fun, but even more so because you caught his passion and energy for what he was doing. Tom was also really funny, and understood the power of humor in creating customer experience.

When we got to some rough parts, where there was not much to see and the kayaking got hard, Tom would have us all either singing, or competing with each other. He had so many ideas just to get us to do something to get us focused off the grind of what we were doing.

All too quickly our trip was over, we were back, and we were loading up the van. Now I will have to admit Tom made that fun too! As we got back on for the forty-five minute ride back, Tom asked us all to share our favorite part of the trip. As we each recalled our favorite parts, again we were laughing, connecting and relating because of this experience. Tom had us engaged the whole way back to the shop. About half way through the ride, Tom asked each of us where we were heading to dinner, and what else we were doing while in Bar Harbor. Again, his knowledge of the area impressed us.

He commented on our choices of restaurants, and mentioned other restaurants we needed to try before our trip was over. Just before we said our final goodbyes, Tom thanked us again and told us he really hoped to see us again. He went on to share all the other great adventures and services that Coastal Adventures provides. He said his favorites were the mountain bikes where we could rent our own or take guided tours, and added that the guided hikes were fantastic. He shared that Coastal Adventures had all kinds of supplies for hiking, mountain biking or just great souvenirs to take home. He said no one leaves Bar Harbor without a Coastal Adventure t-shirt. He also offered, if anyone was interested, to answer questions. He made it clear he would be happy to make sure we got fixed up with the best guides and the best trails.

At dinner that night, with our Coastal Adventure t-shirts in hand, all my husband and I talked about was Tom. Now we had been in Bar Harbor for three days and had done some incredible stuff, but it was Tom and this trip we kept talking about. How incredible it was, how fun it was, and how we were definitely headed back to Coastal Adventures the very next day to sign up to go Mountain Biking (even though we had rented bikes with another group earlier that week).

Again, all in all, Bar Harbor was an amazing trip, and to date, we have probably sent 20 or more people to Bar Harbor, Maine, on vacation, including two of my husband's staff and our best friends. While we don't care where they stay or where they eat, we always, always, always insist they go to Coastal Advetures. We also insist they see Tom. And to this day, we have never had one person come back without telling us how amazing their experience was—they liked Bar Harbor, and they loved Coastal Adventures and they LOVE Tom. They also come home with Coastal Adventures t-shirts.

Everyone we met, worked with and encountered in Bar Harbor did a great job—our hotel, the restaurants, even the shops we went to. We were not the least bit, not the least bit, unhappy with any of it, and if that was all that we had experienced it would have been a good trip. However, the opportunity to experience Coastal Adventures and to experience Tom put that vacation on a whole new level, made it worth remembering and worth talking about.

You see, my husband and I travel a lot, all over the world in fact, and we have had some great vacations. But the vacation we typically talk about is Bar Harbor, and when we do you'll immediately see just what an amazing experience we had. It is written on our faces, our energy changes, big smiles come to our faces, and you better sit back because you are going to hear about Tom. And it is funny to me, that while I have loved all of my vacations, there is not one other place I insist people go, not one other trip, only Bar Harbor, and I will have to admit that when I think about it, that this is sort of crazy to me. Why? Bar Harbor is certainly not the most spectacular place I have ever hiked, or the best mountain biking I have ever done, or the prettiest place I have ever sea kayaked. So why is that the vacation I recommend, why is that the vacation my husband and I talk about? Why is that the one I insist my friends go on, the one I want them to experience? Because that is the power of customer service, and that is the power of you as the CEO of Customer Service.

You see, it is not the meal you eat in the restaurant, it is not the product you buy, or the account you open, but rather the people you encounter that make the difference. How simple that sounds, but how vital and impactful it is. You are sitting there reading this today as professionals, CEOs, business owners, who can and do help people get the products and services they want, but you also have the power to do so much more. As the CEO of customer service you have the ability to help your customers feel supported, watched out for, cared about, and be so much more than just a number. Understand how your customers feel and talk. Then how much they use and refer your company is basically up to you—the result of the experience you have make the decision to provide. The type of experience your customers have is not about the product or service you offer, it is simply about you.

You are the one who makes the difference. You enhance the lives of your customers when you go above and beyond. You may think it is over once your customers buy the product, use your service, or visit your store, but it isn't. If the experience is good, if it is exceptional, it is something that makes them feel good, feel valued and important. Something they want to repeat and something they want to share. Something they will repeat and something they will share.

Now, you need to understand as well, that you also make a difference in people's lives when you don't go above and beyond, when you decide not to be the CEO of Customer Service. If you choose not to provide okay customer service, and choose not to provide an amazing customer service. That is how powerful customer service is and how much it matters in the Trust & Value Economy.

A while ago, I needed to cancel a trip for a "free" training program I had scheduled. The training was "free" (though I had to pay travel and hotel) because I had already paid an annual fee and agreed to purchase a large amount of sales professional and leadership assessments from this organization. Additionally, I agreed to use this company as my exclusive supplier.

Now, this free training is a great service to help those of us who use their assessments to get the most from their investment. I signed up for the course eight months before I was scheduled to go.

Two months prior to my reservation, I needed to reschedule the training. My elderly mother had just experienced a dramatic increase in her memory loss. Though my mother was living in a nice retirement community, these latest episodes were so significant that my sister and I made an agreement that neither of us would be out of town at the same time. Since my sister already had her family vacation planned and had invested quite a bit in this (much needed) vacation, I told her I would take the bullet and stay home feeling certain I could change the training.

I called the company and got the nicest woman on the phone. I explained the situation to her. She was very kind. She listened. She empathized. And then she said she was sorry, but their next training was not until January.

Now, I really did not want to go to Minnesota in January, but what choice did I have? So I told her to sign me up. Then she replied, "Oh no, I do not think you understand. That training is in 2012, and if you do not take the training this year you can no longer represent our company."

A little taken aback at what she said, I laughed. I replied, "I am sorry, I think you just told me that if I do not come in August to this training then I can no longer represent your company." She said "Yes, that is right." Again, I laughed. She said, "I am sorry, I do not understand what is so funny." Shaking my head, I went on to tell her that I made it clear that I cannot come and will not come. And I told her I thought it was funny that she thought she could make me do what she wanted me to do.

I went on to ask her if she had Googled "assessments" on the Internet. And if so, did she notice how many companies sold assessments. And of those, how many sold the exactly the same assessments they sold, complete with this "free" training, customer support and probably some other bell or whistle I did not know about.

In addition, I shared that their sales representative did not inform me this training was required and certainly did not share with me that the training had to be done in the very same year that I signed up to be a distributor. However, he had shared with me that the number of assessments I used ranked very high in my profession and made me eligible for discounts and opportunities within *the company because I was one of their top users and a valued customer.*

I shared with her that I was thinking that maybe, just maybe, her company needed me more as a customer than I needed them as a provider. To make a very long story short, the joke was on me because I spoke with her manager and ended up going to training in Minnesota in January rather than August.

Now, not only was that bad service, it was service that in one tiny phone conversation undid all the effort, time and money the sales representative spent in bringing me to the company.

For those of you reading this who are profit driven (which I hope is most of you), I want to emphasize expense. Remember, it takes approximately six times as much time, money and expense to win me as a customer than it takes to keep me as a customer. Even knowing that, their need to fill training seats was more important than my comfort as a customer.

For me, while I could forgive this mistake on their part, I would not forget it. At that time, my life was just too busy to change vendors or really complain. But within a year, I was gone from that company without a word, without a complaint. And when they called to follow up, I shared my story. They fell all over me to try to make up for it, but it was too late. Why? Because I knew as the consumer that I had a choice. I did not have to spend my money, waste my time or invest any effort in building a relationship with a company that did not prioritize customer service. In the old days, the old economy, when customers got bad service, we got mad, we complained; now we just move on.

In the Trust & Value Economy, your customer is sitting at a buffet of companies that offer exactly what you do. And even if they have loved your dish the best for years, if they put their fork in it one time and the taste is bad, they will move on. Why? Because, it is so easy. Your best customers—the ones you really need to be pleasing—are bombarded every single day with enticing messages, and promises of what another company or sales professional can do for them.

Wake up and smell the coffee, let go of your ego, and put your customer service program into overdrive. Understand? Because, if you do not, you and your company are in serious danger of losing your customers, especially your best customers. Statistics show that 80 percent of customers who leave companies to go somewhere else report that they had a satisfying experience with that former company. Eighty percent!

Just one simple thing

Just like everything else we do in business and in life, we overcomplicate customer service. We make it far more difficult than it has to be. In spite of the number of books that have been written, courses that have been designed and taught, and endless speakers and workshop leaders that have built their careers on customer service, I feel that we have lost sight of what customer service really is. We have turned it into this list of tasks and specific steps that we have to do, an actual checklist in some companies instead of a lifestyle, a way that we live. We have made it an external duty that we do rather than an internal motivation that ignites in ourselves and our teams a care for people. When we train for customer service, we reduce it to a "to do" list, when in reality customer service is extremely personal and unique to the individual. It isn't a 'what we do', it is more of a 'how we do it.'

So really, to learn how to provide exceptional customer service, there is just one thing you need to know, just one thing you need to do, and just one thing you need to understand to make excelling at service easy to do, rewarding to do, and something your customers will talk about to their friends and their neighbours. There is just one thing that you need to know about service that will make your job more fun, easy and effective, and ensure you are the CEO of Customer Service.

To understand the importance of customer service in today's market place, and the value of this one simple thing, you first need to really understand the changes our customers and society in general are experiencing today. In the last twenty years we have lost significant opportunities to connect, interact and engage with others on a day-to-day basis, and that trend is predicted to continue. As we discussed in earlier chapters of this book, we can go home and Google to our hearts content, and buy and shop for anything we want, and never interact directly with another human being. And with technology continuing to advance, and our lifestyles becoming more and more about convenience, this trend of less human interaction is going to continue. In the next decade, it is predicted that we will see our opportunity to connect and engage with one another actually continue to decline.

Think about it. In your own world, your day-to-day activities, you used to go inside a bank and talk to a teller; now you do most of your banking online or at the ATM. We used to go to the bookstore; now we buy via Amazon or other online retailers. And we used to catch up on the local news or gossip with the grocery store clerk; now we use self checkout. Ironically, because we have created a society that demands all of this easy and self-serve style of business, we have become a society that is now hungry, starving for and craving more opportunity to have a meaningful and valuable connection and we want to have a service experience. So when you understand that, when you realize how much experience and human connection have been, and are becoming, more scarce in our society, and you combine it with the fact that availability of product and service are abundant, you realize not only that the customer has a choice, but what is the deciding factor in their decision-making process. That deciding factor is service. You begin to understand why people, our customers, have become far, far less tolerant of mediocre service.

But this is great news for you, the CEO of Customer Service, because you don't provide mediocre service, and while this has always been important, now it is actually a competitive advantage. The more you understand and use customer service as an opportunity, the more of an advantage it will become.

This finally leads us back to the one simple thing we can do to help our customers, our organization, our employees and ourselves. Delivering customer service at the level you want to provide it, boils down to understanding your customers and keeping up with the changing expectations and demands of those customers. Easily said, but keeping up with changing expectations and demands can be tricky. With the knowledge we gained on the challenges our society has created for customers, in terms of the abundance of choices and lack of human connections, we are better positioned to exceed their expectations and create a truly memorable experience. And to create that memorable experience, all we have to do, all we have to remember, is this one simple thing. The one simple thing is to first identify and then fulfill our customers' basic needs. That is it!

If you take little else from this book, then please take and learn this. Your customers are overwhelmed with choice. They can get products and services. What they cannot get, what is being overlooked by your competitors, is their desire to have their basic needs met. If you can learn that, if you can deliver that, if you go through life working to honestly and authentically fulfill the basic needs of your friends, your family, and your customers then you will truly be the CEO of Customer Service. In addition, your relationships will be enhanced, you will give extreme value to those around you, and you will more than exceed your customers expectations. You will leave them "wowed", excited and loyal to you and your company.

Identifying and delivering on the one simple thing

So what is our basic need, what defines a basic need for one customer vs another, and how do we identify the basic need of our customers?

Our customer's basic need and everyone's basic need is simple, it is just to be:

Heard

Acknowledged

Remembered

Respected.

That is it. That is all people—your customers—really want: to be heard and acknowledged, to be remembered and respected. This is the foundation of connection and how you create an experience that is valuable, memorable, and builds trust.

So think about that. Do you want your customers to have a memorable experience, to engage in more of your services, to be longstanding customers who become your advocates sending their family, friends and acquaintances to you? All you have to do is ensure that you consistently and continually fill each one of your customers' most basic need. You and every member of your team, from the person who answers the phone, to the person who handles complaints, to the person who sweeps the floors or fixes the computers, needs to be keenly aware of the importance of the customers' basic need.

Why is filling the basic need so powerful? Because when you do, when you focus your customer service energy there, you emotionally engage with your customer, and you let them know they are important and valuable. The value of service to the customer, the importance of it when it comes to decision making is like sales and like most decisions we as humans make. They are made from an emotional standpoint. Whether we are aware of it or not, we base our decisions far more on how we feel, rather than what is said. Filling a customers' basic need, ensuring they have been heard, acknowledged, remembered and respected, makes them feel important and valuable. It makes them feel far more special at your place of business than they did at your competitor's. Remember it is not the product or service you offer your customers, but about how you offer it.

Filling your customers basic need ensures you create a unique and personal experience for them, one that leaves them wanting to share that experience with others and sends them running back to you for more. So if filling the basic need is so important, what can or should you be doing consistently to meet or exceed this expectation?

The basic need

1: To be heard

You simply begin each and every interaction by asking questions and then really listening for the answer. Never assume you know what the customer wants or needs. A question or two opens the conversation to explore what is truly on their mind, and helps you understand their motivation. My friend in Minnesota was so dedicated to accomplishing her goal, she never bothered to hear my need. Her commitment to getting her class filled left me feeling like she did not care what was going on with me.

2: To be acknowledged

Make sure you call them by name if you know it, if you don't know it, introduce yourself and ask for theirs and then use it. Smile, make eye contact, and let them know they are heard. Nothing is more frustrating, and we have all had the same experience, than to go into a store and no one acknowledges you or even bothers to recognize that you are there. Take Sue from Bar Harbor—the moment she smiled and stepped out from behind the counter, made my husband Rob and I feel like we were the only two people in the store that day. We felt important.

3: To be remembered

There are so many ways we let people know they were remembered. We can certainly do the obvious and welcome them back, remember their name, but beyond that there are lots of little ways that we show people we remember them. When we follow up on something they shared in conversation, or we implement an idea or suggestion that they had made, or even reference something they said in an earlier conversation, all of those show people we remember them. When I arrived in Minnesota for my training in January, not only did no one say a word about what had happened just a few short months earlier, they acted like I had never had a problem with the company or had a care in the world with their service. It told me volumes about where I ranked with them in terms of their caring about my relationship with their organization.

4: *To be respected*

We show people we respect them when we look at them when they talk to us, when we are on time, when we answer their questions, and put their needs above our own. Tom was the king of respect. He could, as many guides do, just simply have told us about our trip and pointed out the various attractions in Bar Harbor, but instead he did it by getting us to share first. He respected our need to be valued and important. In addition, no matter what he was doing, what he was engaged in, he would easily answer a question, double check to make sure we had everything we needed, and make sure that we understood our comfort and our fun were always front and center.

So as the CEO of Customer Service, I want you to be conscious of this the next time someone is in front of you. Whether this person, your customer, realizes it or not, they have a basic need. I didn't realize it at the time, but when I look back on it now, I realize that is what Sue and Tom did—they recognized and filled my basic need. If I were to write the perfect customer service training, and model it after Sue and Tom, I couldn't really do it, because it is too difficult to list a series of tasks or make a checklist. The main reason I can't is because the service was unique to *me*, it met *my* need and *my* expectations, at the same time meeting the expectations and needs of *every other customer* on that trip. The only way to truly provide great service, consistently and continuously, is to meet the basic need of each one of your customers. To ensure they are heard, acknowledged, respected and remembered.

See when we meet the basic need of our customers we take the difficulty out of providing exceptional service. Why? Because our customers will actually tell us how to create a unique experience for them; one that meets their needs and their goals. And by working through the basic need, we create service that is easily adaptable to constant change and continually provides the opportunity for true emotional connection and an experience that not only exceeds expectations but one that is worth its weight in gold in gaining us happy, satisfied, loyal customers who are anxious to become our advocates and referral sources for us.

To keep up, outpace the customers

In the area of customer service, you cannot sit on your laurels. You must consistently evaluate and enhance the level of service you offer. The effort you are putting into retaining customers today is not good enough to keep them next year.

When people set out to make a purchase now, they are interested in the entire experience, not just in taking home a fancy box with a product inside. If your company does not make them feel as though they (and their business) are valued and important, they will move on to another provider who will make the extra effort to give them a positive experience.

Years ago, Nordstrams became famous for their service. Shoppers enjoyed such extras as a live pianist creating a soothing sound throughout the store, and store clerks who expertly packaged purchases and then walked out from around the counter to hand them to their clients and thank them for being a Nordstrams customer.

The experience of service at Nordstrams was so legendary that people would go to the stores just to experience it. Shoppers were known to travel an hour or two just to visit a Nordstrams store. Their service was so famous, that companies in a wide range of industries looked to Nordstrams to model their customer service programs. Yes, in the world of customer service, Nordstrams had arrived.

Even with all that fame, that incredible brand, Nordstrams did not rest on their reputation. They got it! They knew that what they had delivered in the past that had customers traveling to their stores, staying in their stores for hours and spreading the word about their amazing experience, was not going to be enough to "hold" these very same customers going forward.

So Nordstrams raised the bar and took their customer service model into the digital age—where their customer was. They began offering an iPhone app that allowed for sneak peeks at new arrivals, instant messaging about sales and the opportunity to communicate with sales associates directly. Through the app, those associates can "save" items for customers or create a shopping cart specifically for that customer.

Why do all this? Because Nordstrams so perfectly understands that in order to compete, in order to continue to retain their customer base, they need to put customer service front and center.

In today's market, Nordstrams remains a cut above.

You set the tone 24/7

As the business owner, your attitude towards customers and people in general—from your vice presidents to your doormen—signals to the rest of your team how to behave toward customers. And when it comes to customer service, your actions speak far louder than words.

When you were operating on your own, it was easy to decide how you were going to treat your prospects and the types of policies that you'd follow. However, once your business gets to the point where you are recruiting staff, everyone in the organization will take their cue from the way you conduct yourself, regardless of whether or not you are actively engaged in serving or calling on prospects. Your employees will be attentively watching the ways you interact with customers, employees and everyone else in your network.

Whether you see it or not, you are engaging in customer service activities every time you interact with someone else in a professional capacity. It is actually part of your brand; it tells people volumes about you. As a business owner, your character and attitude will shape people's views of your company.

Everyone you have a conversation with has the potential to become a customer of your business, refer you to someone who could become a customer or just talk about your business in the community. As a sales professional in today's economy, how you conduct yourself at the local Rotary, with the waiter on Friday night and with your fellow employees sends clues about how you treat your customers. That's pretty heady stuff, isn't it?

Everyone you meet is connected to a bigger network that may contain possible business prospects. You have no idea what kind of connections the person who serves you at the coffee shop or at the dry cleaners may have, which means that you simply can't afford to be anything less than patient and polite with everyone you meet.

In fact, if people observe a major difference between the way you treat business prospects and your local barista, they may perceive your behavior as a sign of insincerity and dishonesty.

As I said, customer service is on steroids now, and you have to showcase it, whether it is with an existing customer or a potential customer. A little civility will go a long way towards establishing your reputation as someone who is genuinely interested in meeting and exceeding the needs of others.

So, get yourself in check—and then start spreading the message throughout your entire organization.

The sale is for the customer, not you

Let's go back to my poor friend from the training company in Minnesota. How she treated me tells me volumes about where that company places customer service on their priority list.

As a consultant, I could make a strong argument that her responses toward me was not her fault. I have never been to a sales meeting at that organization, but I can tell you what goes on there and what message they are conveying to their employees. The message that reservationist received was that her priority was to get the August training full; do what it takes to get us at capacity. She may have even been promised some incentive to do so.

What was not discussed at that meeting was the need to take care of and really listen to the customer. Figure out what the customer needs and whether or not they can deliver. Do what it takes to make the customer feel heard, important and valued.

Chuck Walker, Vice President of Sales and Marketing at Silver-Line Plastics, credits putting actions behind the words "customers first" with what has kept them exceeding sales expectations during these challenging times.

When the market started to shift, and things began to get tough, Walker knew that service, not price, was the one thing his company had going for it. They had invested years in selling a quality product, standing behind it and being there for their customers. Now, with competition at an all time high, customers more price sensitive than ever, it was time to start "selling" those features, putting them out in front as major benefits of working with Silver-Line Plastics.

"Getting our sales and service departments working together to put the customer relationship first and foremost has been key in our ability to continue to grow in less than perfect economic times," says Chuck. "We have placed major emphasis on ensuring our sales team is well trained and owns the sale from start to finish."

What Walker means by "start to finish" is that he has educated his entire team, invested in training his team and held his team accountable to make sure no matter what—whether it is a sales issue, a service issue or an operations issue—the sales team stays engaged. In addition, he has ensured that the service and operations team have been given training, motivation and support to move more into a sales role. Providing them with the knowledge and support they need to understand how vital is their role in engaging, retaining and deepening the customer relationships.

"This economy, while challenging, has made us a better company

and a better team at every level," reports Chuck. "While we know that things will turn around, on some level we are grateful for the challenges we have gone through, as now we are fully prepared to weather any storm."

And weather it they have. Since this economy started to shift, competition increased, and customers became more price sensitive, Walker and his team have seen growth rates of upwards of 20 percent.

Having the opportunity to work with Silver-Line, I know this happened not only because of Chuck's words and leadership but also because of his actions. He is a man who understands that sales is service, that role modeling begins with him, and that the true path to profitability and growth is through the customer.

Change your definition of sales

As Chuck's story so beautifully demonstrates, sales today more than ever are service to the customer. The more service you provide for the customer, the more you truly help your customer, the more you sell. What could be more noble, more cooperative, more needed than that in today's market of complicated gizmos and endless choices.

However, the average person doesn't define sales as a helping profession—maybe even your own sales team doesn't. All you have to do is say you're in sales and watch people's expressions to know that. That needs to change.

My nephew is a bright, outgoing, funny and good-looking young man. He's someone everyone loves (okay maybe I am a little prejudiced). But he is a natural at engaging people. He realized at an early age that all you have to do is ask people about themselves, be genuinely interested in what they say and a relationship begins to grow. Always one looking to earn a buck, he used to take his guitar to the local gathering spot in his tiny town, open his guitar case and start to play. Believe me, it was his charm not his musical ability that would get the people to gather. The way he told stories about his songs, looked people in the eye and connected with his listeners brought in the tips. In essence, he was selling his talent, selling an experience, and people were willing to pay him for providing that experience.

One day we were sitting around discussing what he was going to do with his life. Now, he loves people, loves a challenge and loves variety, so I suggested to him that he think about becoming a salesperson. By the look on his face, you would have thought I told him to spend his life in prison. He made it very clear to me that there was no way under the sun that he was going to be a salesperson. The last thing he wanted to do was sales. Why? Because for many of us the term "sales people", the profession, just brings bad thoughts.

Now I would like to go on record as saying that I do believe, once my nephew really understands sales, that is what he will grow up to do. I just need to shift his thinking.

In fact, I am on a mission to shift everyone's thinking. What is it about the word "sales?" Why do we dislike it so much? It is the lifeblood of any organization. Sales make the world go round. But it is close to the last job that most people want to take on or admit that they do.

The truth is that people do not like to think of themselves as "in sales." As a society, we just don't like the word or the profession. Most of us like to believe it is someone else's job. However, in the Trust &

Value Economy, if you are breathing, you are in sales. If you want to be successful in this economy, if you want to win, then every member of your organization needs to become a professional sales person.

Put everyone on your team in sales

When I work with organizations developing and training their sales people, I always request to work with their support staff and customer-service professionals as well. My goal is to train everyone to sell and to have everyone understand they are key contributors to the sales cycle.

At first, there is always resistance both from the leadership and from the "non-sales" teams themselves. However, once we talk through this new economy, about what sales really is and how vital their role is in both retaining and developing customer relationships, reason always wins out.

It is a myth that the only people in your organization who are involved in sales are your sales representatives. Though sales professionals do, by definition, lead the way in generating revenue for your business, they are only a part of the equation. Everyone on your team needs to be an active part of this effort.

In fact, in a Trust & Value Economy, the only way to succeed, the only way to truly build a relationship with your customers, is for every member of your team of professionals to be part of the sales cycle. From the first moment that a potential client comes in contact with a member of your organization, you and your employees are forming the very image that customer or prospect will have of your company. Since confidence in your company is an essential component in helping a buyer decide to purchase from you, every interaction at every level, no matter how big or how small, is a sales-related interaction.

In today's economy, silos (isolated departments) within an organization are destructive. Having divisions sectioned off, separated from each other by different goals and different visions, competing against each other, is a negative for the employee, the customer and your business.

Customers are customers of your business—not of certain departments or certain people. That is how your customers see themselves, as customers of your entire business. Oh, we may have labels for departments, but our customers work with our business— period. When customers have an issue, they want it resolved— period. They don't think about calling the service department for service needs or the technical department for operational needs, etc. They just think about having a problem, sharing their story and having whoever they are talking to solve that issue. In addition, as future needs and opportunities arise in their customers' lives, they expect someone, anyone in your organization, to help them continue to enhance and grow their businesses and their lives.

It is impossible for your small sales team to stay on top of all of the changing and expanding needs of your customers. Let's face it, their job is chiefly to bring in new business. Sure they follow up with customers and keep in touch, but really once a prospect becomes a customer, the job of selling to that customer needs to be shared and, quite frankly, owned by the internal members of your team.

So inform your employees who don't view themselves as sales people that they are now on your internal sales team. And then make sure you give them what they need to do the job.

Train everyone to sell at every opportunity

As much as your sales team needs to be actively engaged in service, your service team needs to be actively engaged in sales.

To the customer, both of those tasks feel like "customer care." Because of that, all of your team members must share the same mindset and approach toward keeping customers happy—whether that means servicing their immediate need or helping them find a product to achieve their future goals. I repeat, silos in the Trust & Value Economy are simply destructive to the care of your customer and to the reputation of your business.

As we've already discussed, your customers interact with team members inside your organization all day long. They have service issues, operations issues, maintenance issues. They get advertising and marketing literature, bills and statements, and the list goes on. So the likelihood that a customer, once they become a customer, will interact more often with a member of your internal team than your sales team is pretty high.

These constant and consistent interactions create amazing opportunities to engage your customers in conversations about the challenges and opportunities they are facing and how your organization can help them achieve their dreams. These interactions are the greatest opportunity for you to enhance the customer experience and deepen the customer relationship. Talk about a way to stand out and truly differentiate yourself from the competition!

However, you can only do that if each and every member of your organization understands they are in sales and is properly trained.

In order to get your entire team prepared, invest in sales education and development at every level throughout your organization. Believe me, the effort is more than worth the investment. Imagine doubling, even tripling your sales force. What if every member of your internal team brought one new client to your business? What if they deepened one relationship by selling two or three more products? What would that do to your profits, your sustainability, and your reputation in the community? So where do you start? Begin easy. Start with a skill everyone on your team can get behind and buy into.

Listening is such an important part of selling because your main goal is making sure that you have a clear picture of your customer's needs. This is where you differentiate yourself from your competition, and where you really enhance the customer experience.

Imagine it from your customer's point of view. They have been "sold" by your sales people; they are officially a customer. For them, their experience with most salespeople has been that after that schmoozing to close the deal, the "care" usually stops. Given their experience with most companies, customers are "expecting" that once they become a customer, they will mostly be forgotten about. And, unfortunately, that is usually true.

When I worked in banking, we had studies that indicated that most people were reluctant to change banks because they believed the experience would be just as bad somewhere else. Isn't that sad? Most people tolerate being treated at a level they feel is subpar because they have no faith that another company would treat them any better.

A month ago, I had an unfortunate experience with a company that I knew invested heavily in their marketing budget and sales training. Unfortunately they only trained, I believe, their external sales force. We had just spent a great weekend with good friends at their cabin in the mountains. I wanted to send a thank you in the form of a flower arrangement for the new dining room table our friends had just purchased. Typically, I would call a local florist, but when I began to Google their number I could not find it, and I kept getting the 800 number for this other flower shop (again, smart move they invested heavily in SEO—search engine optimization) so I decided to just call them. They had a great website, it was so easy to find an arrangement that I liked and would work. The nice sales person, helped me get it all worked out and made some fantastic suggestions on an upgrade to a lovely pot and the type of card I should send. I was so happy with my decision.

So imagine how disappointed I was, when a day later I had a message to call the company as there was a problem with my order. The nice service person who answered the phone looked up my order and informed me that the problem was the address I had given was located in too remote a place for most of their providers, and I would need to give them the name of a town or city that was close to my friends' home. Happy to do that, I provided a couple of small towns, and the nice service person assured me all would be taken care of. So again, imagine how surprised I was, when at 5 p.m. that day, they called again saying there was a problem with my order. Again, I called back and again they informed me that they were sorry, and while they assured me they could fill the order none of the small providers they had located could fill an order that large or with those specific flowers. My nice service lady wanted to know if I would be willing to choose another arrangement.

Now I will have to admit, I was getting a little irritated at this point, but I agreed and chose another arrangement. The last straw however came when I got one more call informing me there was a problem; it seems the arrangement that was my second choice was not available either. Again, they wanted to know if I could choose another arrangement. At this point, I informed the customer service person, very nicely I might add, that this was becoming too much trouble and I would rather just go another direction with having my flower arrangement sent to my friends. Oh no she said, please we can take care of it. I said no thank you, again you have been very nice, but this is just not working out this time, I will be happy to use you again when I work in a larger geographical area or city. My request then was just to have them refund my money. To which she replied no, wouldn't I be interested in another arrangement, a store credit, or couldn't there be another option. Again, I repeated what I wanted, but it was like saying it to a brick wall; she just kept asking that I make another choice. This back and forth went on to the point where I was yelling at her (not proud of that) "Can you not hear me? Why aren't you listening? I do not want to do choose another arrangement, I do not want a store credit, I do not want another product, I want a refund and to be allowed to go and get my arrangement somewhere else." Still not listening she went to go and get her manager, and again we went back and forth until finally I asked to speak to someone who could make a final decision.

The end of the story is that I did get my refund after thirty more minutes on the telephone. In addition, I shared with the manager that by not listening to me, he had not only wasted my time and that of his sales people, but he guaranteed that I will never, ever do business with his company again. Had the experience been different I would have. You see I did not care that they did not have the product I wanted or were not able to deliver it where I needed, what I cared about is that they did not listen. By not listening they were completely unable to fill my basic need.

I will venture to guess that this company invests heavily in training, and customer surveys, the secret shopper kind where someone calls in and makes sure that each and every one of your representatives asks the ten questions you have trained them to ask. I could tell by the fact that everyone who got on the phone with me sounded like a broken record, repeating the same sentences and the same questions. They may have passed secret shopper 101 class, but they failed to listen, and meet my most basic need, and in doing so ensured they will never get my business again.

Be the company that excels at customer service

If this is what your customer is expecting, why not be the company that surprises them. Adopt a new approach and engage your entire team in the sales process. Doing so will ensure every interaction this new customer has with your organization, every interaction with your team, is about enriching, enhancing both their relationship with you and the overall goals of their company. Every member of your team understands and knows how to go further with the customer, to do more than just handle the issue the customer has called about.

If that flower shop/company had bothered to train their inside team as heavily as they were training their external team they would see amazing results in terms of return on investment in customer retention, growth and depth of products and services used. In addition, they would ensure that the very large amount of money they have to be spending to remain top of the list on the search engines, is being turned into profit when customers call in to make a purchase.

Salespeople can be the hardest sell

While you are investing in education for the "internal" sales team, be sure to continue to develop your external team as well. For many of us in sales, the way we learned to sell in the old economy has become a habit and one that takes education and awareness on our part to break. I am continually amazed as I work with sales teams across the nation how ingrained it is in us to put ourselves first and our customers last. We may understand intellectually that this is sure financial ruin in today's economy, but changing our actions is another story.

> I was leading a networking workshop in Washington, D.C., and the whole goal of the event was to help salespeople understand how to build a powerful network. We spent two hours discussing, role playing and going through techniques on how to invest in others first, add value and give without expectation of return. We discussed how to use patience to your advantage and invest in others before you ask them to invest in you.

> When the workshop was over, a man in the class came up to me and said, "I loved the class. Thank you. Now I would love to get together with you and tell you a little about what I do. Given your connections, I think what I do is a perfect fit for many of your clients."

I just had to laugh. Did he not hear anything we just discussed? Did not one single role play or real-life example stick? Did not one part of this workshop help him understand that by asking for what he wanted before bothering to learn what I wanted did nothing but ensure there is no way I want to be part of his network or include him in mine?

My point is that salespeople have been trained for so long on how to "win" at sales that many of them treat the "sell" like a sporting event. We see our goal to defeat the other "team." Well, that other team is our customer. And to make the sale in the Trust and Value Economy, we have to help customers make their goals. We're partners. We win when they win.

Sales and service are one

If your entire staff understands that their primary purpose is to proactively serve the needs of your customer by uncovering opportunities to build and enhance the relationship, then the lines between selling and service will become almost invisible. Your silos will officially be gone.

It really all comes back to putting your customer's needs first, which should be the guiding rule for anyone who is in business in this economy. Your company exists because your products or services are capable of meeting the real, important needs of your customers and your prospects. Helping your team to see themselves as partners in a wide, mutually beneficial network with your customers will encourage them to not only seek to understand the issues clients face but also to look for ways in which your company can be a part of the solution.

KEY TAKEAWAY

To win in a Trust & Value Economy, become the CEO of customer service. Every department in your enterprise is the sales department, every employee a salesperson.

CHAPTER 7

Plan for Change

I am by nature an optimist. I do see the glass as half full. I am one of those annoying people who believe that challenges create opportunity and obstacles just call for more persistence and creativity. However, by nature of what I do for a living, I am also a realist. And in this economy, even for the most optimistic of us, the new reality is tough. The constant shifting of the economy promises to create an even more challenging road ahead.

That's not to say (I am an optimist after all) that these can't be your best years on record. I caution you, however, that you need to be prepared. If you want this economy to yield some of the most successful times you have experienced, then you need a plan. In times like these, it is those businesses that have a plan, build their skills, and know how to remain flexible that will enjoy success.

We all know the statistics for business success in any economy are daunting. Most businesses fail in the first five years. And among the ones that make it, few ever reach a level of economic security. Stress, anxiety and worry are often the constant companions of the business owner.

But here is the good news. Many of the reasons businesses succeed, struggle or fail are under our control as business owners. That remains true even in the toughest business environments. We have the power to gain the knowledge, make the decisions and take the steps to ensure we succeed. The trick is we have to actually "do it."

If you look back on history, there have always been times of economic struggle. But there have also always been businesses, professionals and entrepreneurs who not only survived but thrived in that struggle. Their success was rooted in their ability to be proactive, take action, remain focused and navigate troubled times, rather than be a victim to circumstances.

Create a map to success

So it's well within your ability to be one of those success stories in these troubled times. Start with a plan of action that covers these areas:

1. **Strategy**—Form a clear vision of where you want your business to be a year from now and write it down. Beneath it, write out—step-by-step—how you plan to reach that vision. What are your goals? What behaviors will you follow? How will you measure and keep track of your progress? How will you hold yourself accountable? Having a strategy will go a long way to ensure you remain focused, on task and consistently moving your business forward. A tough economy allows no room for wasted energy, time or resources. You have a lot coming at you, and if you do not know where you want to go, every path is going to sound good.

Without a strategy, you likely will find yourself standing in the same spot you are standing in right now, looking like a deer in the headlights.

2. **Marketing/Sales**—Define a sales and marketing process. You need a consistent plan that includes actions for generating new customers, retaining existing customers, and building a brand and reputation that increases your referrals. At the top of your to-do list in the plan should be proactive client contact on a daily basis. Losing sight of promoting your business can be devastating to your ability to grow, let alone sustain your business. All too often business owners and professionals get too busy doing other things to worry about making sales calls or contacting "satisfied" customers. They, wrongly, believe that if people want something they will contact them. Remember in this economy, getting them to choose you, and continue to come back to you, takes effort.

3. **Budget**—To grow a business, you have to be in command of how much money flows in and out of that business on a monthly basis. (And I think everyone who works in the business should understand cash flow.) Once you have a handle on your cash flow (income and expenses), turn your focus to future and expected growth. Determine how much money you want to make. Then go back to your marketing and sales strategy and make sure it supports your projected budget. Sales/marketing and budget strategies need to be connected! Then, each month, spend time analysing your income and expenses, your cash flow. In addition to keeping you financially healthy, staying on top of cash flow will give you great insight into how your daily actions positively or negatively impact your bottom line. Then you can adjust your actions accordingly for success.

4. **Systems**—Repetition and consistency are important to business success – not sexy but true. Once you have established what is working in your business, systematize your process: how products are made, services are delivered, customers are contacted, and how goals and sales are recorded and measured. Systems improve communication, create efficiency, and make hiring and training employees/contractors a far easier process. More importantly, they create consistency for customers. A key to trust is the guarantee that each and every experience your customer has with you will be as good as or better than the experience before. Systems give you a way to ensure you can provide that level of experience.

5. **Accountability and support**—It is lonely at the top. Business owners and professionals need support to build and maintain their confidence and to keep them focused and accountable. As business owners, we are responsible for everything, so it is easy to get sidetracked and pulled away from our priorities. Accountability is critical to success. When we hold ourselves accountable, we provide valuable information and opportunity to learn about ourselves and our businesses. Accountability shows us what we are doing well and where we are struggling. It can help us see what we can do to improve. If you are a professional who works for a business, then waiting on others to hold you accountable is a sure fire way to discover you have already lost out. Leaders are the people everyone else comes to—our employees, our customers and our vendors. It seems everyone needs our energy and our time. By having a coach, a peer group or a mastermind, you can both get the support you need to remain on task and focused, as well as get the motivation you require to run your business.

6. **Radical customer focus**—This step is the foundation upon which all other steps in your strategy sit. Every step of your plan must be created with your customer's needs first in your mind. Remember the slogan James Carville coined for Bill Clinton's campaign, "It's the economy, stupid." Well to build a successful business today, change that to, "It's the customer, stupid." Keep your focus squarely on your customer.

Plan for a longer sales cycle

As you develop your overall strategy, take into account the longer sales cycle in the Trust & Value Economy. As you move through this book, you will learn why and how to build trust and a strong relationship with each client. While this effort will pay off in spades, it does take time. In addition, as we talked about in Chapter 3, today's customers are more cautious with their money, have more choices about where to buy and want to do their research before they buy. Again, this takes time and slows the sales cycle.

However, if you try pushing your customer, you'll quickly come to the end of the sales cycle, and not with the result you were hoping for.

> A case in point: I was checking into a hotel in California, and I was tired. I had been on the road more than a week, speaking and consulting. I pulled into the hotel after a long day of driving from Northern to Southern California. All I wanted to do was check in, get to my room, grab something to eat and head to bed. The hotel was five-star and looked amazing.
>
> As I walked up to the check-in desk the clerk did everything right: big smile, called me by name, etc. He pulled up my account only

to discover that I am not a rewards member or whatever loyalty program they were hosting. He immediately jumped at the chance to sell that to me. I politely declined. But he insisted. I declined again. And again he insisted, happily saying it would take only 30 seconds. I was livid, but I gave in.

Now, I was not mad because he got me to sign up for the product, I got mad because it was so clear this relationship was not about me. He was clearly not listening. Not listening to my words, and not paying attention to the clues that this was not the time to be selling to me. He was completely oblivious to what I wanted as the client. (Now I will admit that because my field is developing customer focus, companies that do not train or develop these skills in their people really upset me.) The poor clerk took no notice (and I would venture he was not trained to) of what was going on with me as the customer (I was tired and wanted to go to my room). It was clear his focus was on a required goal that he needed to hit by month's end. Sure he made the short-term sale. But long-term, I will never choose or recommend that hotel. And my client, who has a corporate account, changed hotels. That may sound harsh, but it isn't. You see there are six five-star hotels within a mile of their company. If the experience is less than par at one, why not change? Isn't that free commerce, isn't that competition at its best?

Patience is a virtue in this economy—make space for it in your plan. Your plan should allow you to balance your need for cash flow with the consumer's need for a slower pace. The new reality for business owners and professionals is that you will need to get comfortable with a longer sales and relationship cycle. In order to develop business and grow sales, you will need to spend a great deal more time with prospects. You still have the ability to influence the buying cycle, but rest assured it is your customers that are controlling it.

Plan to keep your current customers current

Let me ask you this: If you had to make a choice between looking for a large group of customers who you would be able to sell to once or a smaller group of loyal customers who will buy from you time and time again, which group would you want to target? Easy question right? You would target the smaller group.

This is a no-brainer. It's much easier to sell to an established customer base than to be constantly looking for new clients. In the sales world we call this the low hanging fruit, but in the new economy we call it business rooted in trust and value.

When competition is high, like now, and consumers are in control, the worst mistake you can make is to take your current customer base for granted. Even just assuming that because they had a good experience they will come back is a mistake. The quality of your current customer base's experience, and the way in which they tell others about that experience, sends a strong message to future customers about whether or not they will be happy doing business with you.

In this new economic reality, your existing customer base is your bread and butter. This is where you have already done the work, invested your time, and shed your blood, sweat and tears. These are people who are familiar with your brand and who trust that it will help them solve a problem and enhance their business. They are in essence already sold on you. Make it part of your plan to spend time, effort and resources building relationships and adding value to existing customers.

Have a follow-up plan

After you have earned a customer's trust and sold the first product or service, the work does not stop there. You are just getting started. Now, you will need a plan to maintain and grow the relationship. It's important for you as a business owner and a sales professional to be thinking of how you can bring value to your customers to let them know how much their business is appreciated. Even something as simple as keeping in touch can give a customer the confidence they need in the product or service you can provide

A plan for following up and following through is important for both current clients and prospects. You should always be thinking of how you can bring value to your customer or your prospect and let them know you are genuinely interested in their success, whether you are actively selling to them or not.

Let me give you an example:

A while ago, I was on site with one of my favorite clients, a manufacturer in South Carolina. During a dinner meeting with the CEO and CFO, I heard a great sales story. My client had been looking for a new insurance provider. It seems that the company they had worked with for years sold out to a larger organization and their account was now being handled out of Texas. My client really wanted a firm with an office in their state and a representative they could meet with in person. It sounded reasonable, so they started taking bids and interviewing providers.

This is where the story gets good. After two months they narrowed it down to three candidates. They were close to a decision when out of nowhere they landed two big contracts. All of a sudden, human resources, the department overseeing this insurance decision, was

swamped with recruiting, hiring and training new staff to handle the new jobs. Needless to say, the urgency of finding a new insurance provider fell right to the back of the line.

Six months later, when the dust had settled and the new staff were in place, human resources was once again focused on finding a new provider. This time the decision was easy. By the end of this whirlwind of activity, it was clear to them there was just one choice. Only one out of the three providers in the running bothered to stay in touch throughout this period, to follow up.

The winning salesperson kept her name in front of her potential prospect in ways that added value and built the relationship during this downtime—things such as sharing pertinent information and showing support without pushing for the sale. When her prospect, my client's company, was ready to make a decision, she and her firm were top of mind in a way that put her head and shoulders above her competitors.

If you want to outsell your competitor then you need to use every opportunity to build the relationship with the client. You need to keep in touch. You need to follow up.

I know it is not exciting, but quality follow-up is one of the most powerful and easiest ways to outsell your competitors. Research tells us that less than 81 percent of sales people make less than three follow-up contacts with a prospect. Yet research also shows us that most prospects buy after the seventh contact. (I believe that this is even higher now, because of the shift in our economy.)

Most sales people "give up" for a number of reasons, including because they have decided the prospect is not interested or they simply don't want to be annoying. Two understandable reasons, but two very bad assumptions.

The point is, as salespeople, we really don't know why a hot prospect suddenly goes cold. More often than not it has nothing to do with us. There could be any number of reasons why a prospect disengages, reasons that involve other aspects of their life, not their lack of desire or need for the products or services we offer. Perhaps a bigger priority came up at work. They have a family issue. Or they simply got behind due to a vacation or holiday. Who knows?

People are busy. And rarely is what we are selling at the top of their priority list. The sales person who is proactive, who makes it easy for the prospects, and continues to use follow-up as an opportunity to build the relationship, is the sales professional who will win the business.

Plan to be invaluable, not annoying

You are only annoying if you are making the follow-up contact about you and not about them. Too often, our follow-up systems consist of sending an email or calling every 30 days to ask if they are ready to make a decision. We follow up in a way that sends a message that conveys through our actions that we are far more interested in achieving our goal of closing the sale than finding a solution to their issues.

To follow-up effectively you need to keep the focus on the prospect, and follow these three simple steps:

1. **Design a process**—Put a process in place that reminds you when to follow up and who to follow up with. Be sure it can maintain important notes and ideas you learn from each contact.

2. **Make it personal**—Follow-ups need to be customized to the current client or prospect. Too often I see follow-up processes that are just that—a one size fits all. Follow-up is about building the relationship and establishing trust. It is about their needs, not your sale.

3. **Add value**—Follow-up is the time to show your customer or client just how valuable you can be to them. Use it to send an article with information about a challenge they are facing or an opportunity for them. Give them tickets to events they have expressed interest in. Or introduce them to people they would benefit from knowing. Adding value ensures your client enjoys and benefits from the follow-up process.

My client's new insurance provider did not win the business because she is smarter, had a better product or quoted a rock-bottom price. She outsold her competitors simply by following up. So don't give up on your customers, give them value.

I believe in practicing what I preach, so you will find that everything I am telling you about and sharing with you in this book, I do and act on in my own business and follow-up is a huge part of that. Much as I do not want to at times, I always follow up.

However, this past year I had a client I had done two speaking engagements for. For the first I had had a great follow-up session with them, but the second—well, busy schedules on both of our parts and the addition of a new expansion on theirs, had pushed more than one of our scheduled follow-up meetings off the schedule. Here we were six months past the event, and we had still not met with them. We had emailed a few times, and actually spoken on the phone once, but we had not had the official follow-up, which is a hard and fast rule of mine.

At this point, though, honestly what was the point? They were happy, and there was no more business there for me on my part, so why go through the motions. But true to my word and my practice (thinking "How can I look my clients in the eye and tell them they have to do this when I don't") I scheduled the appointment. We had a great meeting, talked about what went well, what challenges they were having implementing some of the things we'd discussed at the sales rally (and they were having no problems—this is a truly terrific team) and as I was just winding down, and getting ready to go, the CEO asked if I was available to do their next Sales Rally.

Now you could have knocked me over with a feather. Are you kidding me, a third? And three years in a row? Turns out they really liked some of the strategies I had presented, and they wanted to change up their format from more of a keynote to more of a workshop. Their team was so interested in the personality testing and profiling fun we had had as it related to team building and building customer connections. The leadership wanted to know if I could do a presentation, a workshop so to speak, on that particular strategy. Of course, I said, and smiled as I thought, "Wow! I just learned a lesson, follow-up really works".

Put your plan in writing, but not in stone

Put your entire plan in writing, from strategy to follow-up. That will ensure you have a clear vision of where you are headed and how you intend to get there.

As you begin to write down your plan, keep in mind that gone are the days of five-year plans. Today's strategies need to be examined far more often, questioned on a routine basis, and updated almost on a quarterly basis.

More than ten years ago, I became a master certified strategic planner. When I first entered the field, we were taught to take a long-term approach. We designed plans that lasted five years for traditional companies and three years for those that thought of themselves as progressive.

In today's market, trying to plan and live that plan for three to five years would not only be difficult but would be somewhat of a waste of time. Think about how much has changed in the last five years in our businesses.

Today's strategic plans call for a new approach, as we discussed. The experts still strongly advise we have a plan and take a long-range view; however today's business needs to be prepared to update, change and enhance their plan every three to four months.

In addition, plans now need to be more externally focused and far more flexible. If you need a strategic plan that is externally focused and far more flexible, don't you need to run your business that way too? Let go of traditional thinking. Let go of the ego you attach to ideas and initiatives, and be open to learning continually and from everyone you come in contact with.

KEY TAKEAWAY

To win in the Trust & Value economy, create a plan that keeps you focused on your customers, focused on exceeding expectations, and focused on achieving and surpassing your goals.

CHAPTER 8

Standing Still Is Moving Backwards

As we've seen in the Trust & Value Economy, the one thing we can count on is change itself. Change, ironically, is consistent. If your goal is to remain in business, then you don't have the luxury of remaining stagnant. Today's businesses need to keep moving and pushing to the next level. Why? Because the value you offer today is not going to be good enough or strong enough to ensure your success going forward.

In this economy, an insatiable curiosity is a major asset. A "can't sit still" personality is a plus. As a business owner or sales professional, your role is to consistently question what you do and what you offer, and use that information to dig deeper, to identify ways to make it better, take it up a notch, and improve the efficiency of your company and the customer experience. Just because it was a hot seller last year, does not mean it is right for your customers today. You need be taking a perpetual inventory of your business, your processes, your customers and your competition, and really question what is working in your company and what is not.

While you are taking that inventory, be sure to include who is working and who is not. Customers, employees, vendors? Business today needs to be earned and earned repeatedly. Gone are the days of loyalty just for the sake of being loyal.

Ride the wave

Try looking at your business as though it is a living, breathing thing. That may sound a little out there, but I believe that how things work in nature has much to teach us about business and life. Let's take a lesson from the great white shark. In fact, imagine your business as a great white shark. Did you know that this ancient species must keep swimming or it will die? Great whites are in constant motion. They cannot stop moving; they have to be constantly pushing forward no matter what the obstacles are. Adaptation is a necessity, not a luxury to the great white. It is a part of the shark's basic survival instincts.

In the Trust & Value Economy, your business shares this characteristic. If you want to keep growing your business, you must be constantly anticipating and responding to changes in circumstances within your organization as well as outside of it. You must push forward and adapt to the changing waters ahead so that your business remains at the top of the food chain and does not suffocate from stagnation. Change is part of the basic survival needs of your business.

Being open to change includes being constantly aware and open to making changes according to your customers' and prospects' constant fluctuations. You have to be ready to react or better yet anticipate their need to turn on a dime and change their priorities. You must constantly make adjustments to what you are offering the people you are selling to, as well as how you are delivering products and services to them.

At every turn, you will need to consider how your actions are benefiting your customers if you want to build on your previous success. Attracting and retaining customers is really just like every other relationship—you have to work at it.

Playing it safe can kill you

There are so many variables in this economy right now that no expert can give you the answer as to exactly what is going to happen. Being willing to do things differently from how you did them before is essential. I would say this is one of the most difficult transitions successful people are having in today's economy. And I get it. If what you have done got you to where you are today, and you have been wildly successful, it is uncomfortable and hard to let go and try something new, to take a risk. However, this economy is all about risk.

Ironically, one of the best examples I have seen of this is with the CEO of an accounting firm. Yes, I said accounting firm. And yes, I am talking about radical innovation. Ben Hamrick is CEO of Johnson Price and Sprinkle, PA (JPS), a regional accounting firm that is growing and expanding despite a challenging economy. Ben and his team are cutting-edge. A committed group of leaders and senior shareholders that have committed to a common vision and a shared set of values. They have taken the challenges of working in a tough economy and turned them into major opportunity. They have done so by being open to change and committed to innovation.

Honestly, I am not sure I know or work with a CEO who is more introspective and questioning then Ben Hamrick. He has to be the poster child for someone willing to take a look at his company from the client's perspective, the associate's perspective and the external market's perspective. I believe that introspection, and his team's willingness to look internally, first comes from their drive to be committed to the client. As a team, they are driven by the belief that if they first serve the client, put their needs ahead of the firm's, that ultimately success will come to both parties.

And they analyzing almost everything they do, focusing on what services they can provide to their clients, and truly being the best at delivering is how they achieve their purpose of "client first." Ben has used the information he has learned from thinking through these various perspectives to transform his organization into one that is truly client-focused and dedicated to the development and growth of his associates. While definitely bottom-line focused, his path to increasing and driving that bottom line and building a healthy company is thinking about how various processes impact the customer, the associate and the market.

Ben and his team believe that when they make decisions that enhance the client and the community first, that this is the strongest way to grow the future of JPS. I believe Ben will go down as a true game-changer in the field of accounting and financial services.

Three strategies to help you change your game

1. **Helicopter View**—Get your leadership team together. Do it now and set aside a half-day or a couple of hours to brainstorm. Take a look at your business from a helicopter view. Take this time to stop working in your business and start working on it. Talk about what is going on with your company, your customers,

and your team. Have an honest, deep discussion about what you are doing that is producing results, and more importantly, what is not. Question why you are still doing what is not, and brainstorm on how to change. Leave this session with three new actions and execute them.

2. **Customer View**—Twice a year, at least, walk through your company as a customer. This is critical, especially if you are in leadership. What is it like to be your customer? What is easy about working with you? What is not, and what needs to change? How could you move your team from providing service to providing an experience?

3. **Outsider View**—Get a coach, a mentor, or a mastermind group. It does not matter, just find someone, some group, any skilled, professional outsider who can push you to look at your business objectively, hold you accountable, and support you in your efforts to question your routine and try new strategies and initiatives. The most successful people understand they cannot do this alone.

Use the ebb to increase the flow

With a strategy on how to identify changes and see them coming firmly in place, let's go back to the ocean for a moment, only this time we will stay on the surface. It may be helpful to think of the changes you are going to encounter as though they were waves and you are a surfer riding them. Just like a surfer, you don't get to choose the waves, how big they are or even when they will come. You have to look for them, prepare for them, and then be open to riding them to wherever they are going to take you. Resist a wave and it will clobber you, ride the wave and you will move forward. The challenge is that you cannot know with any kind of certainty where you will wind up.

When a change is coming in, you will be riding one wave after another on your virtual surfboard, sometimes making decisions on the fly on the best way to keep your business afloat. The waves may pick up suddenly or you may be able to see them breaking from a mile away. Your advantage is that you know and are prepared for the waves that will come, even if you don't know when they will come or how large they will be. Just as waves ebb and flow, changes will come and go. Be sure to use the calmer times to focus on improving procedures or fine tune operations. Learn what you can from past mistakes and successes.

A little preparation combined with knowledge can ensure that the wave takes you on an amazing ride. When you are faced with a sales situation in which you are called on to change something, picture yourself on that surfboard. You may feel a sense of anticipation, unbalance and even a little bit of fear. The experience may be challenging, but it will likely be exhilarating too. And that is the way to embrace change so that you benefit from the experience. No two waves are the same, but riding them out and adapting to their differences will make you an expert surfer in no time. You'll find that your sales improve too.

Stand on your own two feet

It can be tempting to try to chase a particular wave and implement strategies that you've seen are successful for your competition. This may seem like a safer way to do business, but it is not. Playing catch up and following others' paths can be a recipe for disaster. The best way for you to be a leader in your niche market is for you to work with your team and your experts to decide where, when and how to innovate.

You should still keep an eye on what is working well for your competitors. But your top priority should be keeping your fingers on the pulse of the developing issues of your existing customers and their external environment.

In the Trust & Value Economy, your best source of information lies in understanding your customers. Copying something that a competitor is doing well will rarely pull any of their customers towards you, but it might divert your energy from meeting the needs of your previously established clients. In fact, I feel sure it will divert your energy.

It used to drive me crazy when I worked in the world of corporate banking how often we would implement strategies and ideas that we saw other firms and banks implement and then get lackluster results. Now it didn't bother me so much that we would use the idea, but that we would use the idea without thinking it through, without analyzing it, or trying a different approach for delivery or marketing or overall purpose. We didn't listen to the customer or learn from them as to why the product or service our competitor was delivering didn't work or was not accepted by that customer. We lost major opportunities, and wasted valuable resources all because we were unwilling to be introspective.

If you maintain good relationships, strong and proactive contacts with your customers, and you're really listening, you will be able to anticipate ways in which your company can provide for their future business needs. You'll discover ways to innovate and to change; you will make strong, well-educated decisions that will mitigate the risk you feel at trying something new. As long as you continue to provide your customers with the types of products and services they need to meet their evolving desires, you will be well positioned for continued business success.

My husband's dental practice just had a record year. The best success both in terms of patients' outcomes, employee retention and financial results he has had since he opened the doors more than twenty-five years ago. Now, all this despite the fact that many in the dental profession are struggling right now, and dental care is one of those services that people determine is optional in struggling financial times. Most people would prefer to go on vacation or get a flat screen television than go to the dentist.

However, by being willing to shake things up, do things differently, and take a long hard look not only at the services they are providing but how they are providing them, made all the difference. First, they spent time really listening to their customers. Undergoing focus groups, initiating surveys, and spending time in the exam room to ask a question or two. What they learned was time was critical to people; there just was not enough of it these days, and even for those patients who wanted to come to the dentist, finding the time was difficult. In addition, saving money was important to people too, and while they expected to pay for their dental care, it was not an expense they got excited about or felt they truly understood the value of. Lastly, for most of their patients unfortunately, dental care was something they felt they could do without. Yes, my husband and his team learned a lot from spending time engaging with patients. They learned a lot about what they needed to change and shake up at their dental practice.

So that is exactly what they did! First thing they did was walk through the patient experience from phone call to check in to patient exam. They identified and found every single spot and place where they, as service providers, were inefficient. The result? They were able to reduce the patient exam time by more than twenty-five to thirty percent. In addition, they turned Rob's office into a workroom for patients. As he is rarely in there, they set up the computer and the phone so it was available to professionals who needed space to work while waiting for their dental work to finish or the next procedure to be set.

Next, the team invested in learning new procedures and techniques, high-tech based, that provided exceptional dental care in a fraction of the time—techniques such as new procedures for dental implants and dental crowns, where the dentist and his team could deliver amazing dental care in about half the time. This new technology and equipment allowed for crowns to be made in an hour and dental implants in less than a day. It was revolutionary and just what the patient had asked for.

Lastly, they invested in training on how to talk with, educate and share with patients the value of dental care, and more importantly, preventative dental care. If patients kept their regular dental appointments, did the small preventative care each time it was suggested, over the long run they would wind up with healthy teeth, a healthier wallet, and a strong happy smile that would last a long time.

Yes, taking the time to get introspective, and make changes, shake things up a bit, really pays off in a Trust and Value Economy.

You need to be open in this economy, to shed your ego, and to let go of ideas and opinions of doing it "your" way. Feeding your curiosity with continuous learning will put you on a path to becoming a leader in this new world. The better informed you are, the more you listen to your customers, the more open you will be to recognizing and implementing new and innovative ideas.

Shaking it up is the name of the game in this economy. Who knows what the landscape will look like a year from now. But the one thing you do know for sure is that if you stand still you will be in for a serious struggle. So just get on board and embrace this new reality. After all what do you have to lose? You just might learn to find the comfort in chaos.

KEY TAKEAWAY

To win in the Trust & Value Economy, keep moving, never stand still. Prepare yourself and your business to understand the currents and successfully ride the waves of change.

CHAPTER 9

Strengthen Your Foundation—Know Who You Are

If your business does not have a firm foundation, finding success in the Trust & Value Economy is going to be a constant struggle, if not impossible. Now that you truly understand the new reality of the marketplace, it's time to begin to lay the groundwork that will serve as a platform for long-term, sustainable success.

Define your business deliberately

Authenticity is vital in this type of economy, so you need to understand what your business stands for, what the overall purpose of your organization is. And rather than looking for something outside of your business to define you, begin by looking inward.

First determine what both you and your business stand for. Take your time. Craft a well thought-out statement of what matters most to your organization, what you stand for. You can call this your mission statement.

Then define your business's values. Your values are your priorities in action. They are the way you carry out that mission and how you run your business.

If you get this far in the process, you will be far ahead of most in the business. Just knowing what you do, why you do it and how you do it with certainty can catapult you to new levels of success.

If you don't deliberately define your business's mission and values, they will be defined for you. Whether you realize it or not, each and every enterprise, including yours, already has its own personality. It naturally reflects the values on which your team is placing its priorities.

As a business owner and as a professional, if you want your company and your team to reflect your values, then you need to clearly define and state your values. Make it clear to everyone, including employees and customers, how you run your business.

Values speak louder than words

Are the values your company is currently projecting, the values you want to project or not? Do they align with who you and your company are, what you prioritize? Do the values you state and the values act out align? In other words, do you practice what you preach?

The values of your company, defined or not, send a message. They tell your customers, your employees and partners who you are, what you stand for, what is most important to you and how you make decisions.

Values are powerful. They express themselves in how you provide services, how you treat people, and in how employees exhibit the code of conduct. They tell the world what is most important to your business. Again, whether you intend it or not your business already has a personality. It already has values and some type of image. That personality and those images are sending the message of what you value.

Take some time to uncover what your values are. Values and personality come from within. They should be "uncovered" as they already exist in your organization. To be authentic, it is important that you discover (rather than create) what you are, what you are about and what your business stands for. Once identified and defined, your values will provide a strong foundation to your success. Align your everyday deeds with your values and you can't help but distinguish your business from your competitor's.

Values, when they are lived and practiced, and when they truly reflect the owners and employees of that organization, are one of the strongest ways to build trust.

My husband and I travel quite a bit with Backroads, an adventure travel company. If you know anything about the company or talk with any of their employees, you will quickly learn that customer service is job one, bar none their most important value.

Their goal is to "spoil" their customers. They want anyone who travels with them to have an amazing experience. And believe me they live their values. If you ever take a Backroads trip, you will be hard pressed not to walk away having had one of the best vacations of your life. From the time you arrive, anything you want, anything you need, the guides will find a way to make it happen, every time.

Now, why is this important? Because that "living" of their values makes us trust Backroads, and it takes the cost of the trip off the table. We have tried other companies that touted the same values. They provided a good experience but not a great experience, not a customer-service value experience. The result, no matter where we travel in the world, is that we go every single year only with Backroads. And we recommend Backroads to everyone. Why? They clearly define and live their values.

It's not what you do, but how you do it

Your foundation—your mission and your values—is powerful and vital to your success. In the "old" economy, companies were defined more by what they made. In the Trust & Value economy, we are defined more by how we deliver, service and stand by what we make. To be successful in this economy, you need to understand that it is less about what you do and more about how you do it. Business owners who clearly define, live and promote the personality of their company can turn it into a strategic platform that naturally attracts and retains customers, customers who care more about relationship than they do about price.

Marissa Levin, CEO of Information Experts, an award-winning professional with an award-winning company, built the concept that people and culture drive success. Marissa and her company are an amazing example of the power of values. When the economy began to shift, so did Marissa. She set out to remake her company. This was a gutsy move on her part. She began with looking inward and uncovering her values. She sat down with her core team, and took an in-depth look at who they were, what they were about, and what they stood for, looking first to what was most important to them, and what they most wanted to accomplish.

With that work completed, they started to investigate everything about the company, from process, structure, strategy, employees and leaders, to see what was working, and what was not—meaning what aligned with their values and what did not. Anything that did not align had to go. Talk about strongly living your values!

Marissa describes it as the most incredibly difficult thing she has ever done, but truly the most impactful. The company started to run with greater ease, freeing Marissa to start company number two, Successful Culture.

Successful Culture is Marissa's platform to connect with and coach other leaders who believe that a values-based culture fuels growth. Through Successful Culture, Marissa published her first book, *Built to SCALE: How Top Companies Create Breakthrough Growth Through Exceptional Advisory Boards.* The book profiles, and provides working templates for, Marissa's patent-pending model, SCALE™ (Select,

Compensate, Associate, Leverage, Evaluate/Evolve/Exit), which leads business owners through the process to create an advisory board of experts that can drive growth. In her book, she discusses the need to find advisors who not only align with a company's industry and products/services, but also align with a company's value system.

Advisors are an important extension of an organization. They must support and publicly live the company values when representing the company. Yes, values are the heart of your organization and, in the age of authenticity, a must for the Trust & Value Economy.

Ensure your employees share your values

A few months ago, a client of mine fired their new web developer not because the web developer did anything wrong, but because they and their employees simply did not understand, deliver or live the web developer's values.

Strike one

My client paid $10,000 in full for a new website and, as required, he paid in advance. It took three weeks (after payment) for the employees of the company to follow back-up with my client to get started. (You see after the web developer sold the project, he turned the execution of the website over to his team, a team I am assuming he felt would deliver to his standards. The first meeting was scheduled with the web developer's team and the web developer himself was not going to be in attendance. However, my client was informed that if he, the owner of the company, did not attend this meeting, my client would have to agree to pay for additional hours of production that might be required if he had any additional or *different thoughts after the meeting. In fact, he was told that all decisions at that meeting were final, and that even if he did attend, any additional changes he requested would result in additional time charged. While all of this was okay, my client did note that he was not informed of this when he paid what he thought was $10,000 universal charge for a new website. As far as values go, this was strike one!*

Strike two

Second, my client was then asked to fill out a standard online information form to get started. In addition he was told that if he had questions to simply call or fill in the ask the Q&A form available on the site. Great! Only it took three work days to get an answer back either way, from a call or from the online form. Strike two.

Strike three

Due to the unanswered questions, my client missed their deadline to have the form returned so the site could not now be started at the previously scheduled time. No phone call, no check in and no "can we help you call" from the web developer ever occurred. The client's feeling? You have my money and you don't really care if and when I get started. Strike 3

The result? My client, nicer than he should have been, tried with no avail to get the help he needed. With no luck, he asked for his money back, a full refund. Here comes the web developer, the owner of the company again. Now the web developer started to add value, exhibit his values, build trust and even offered discounts all in an *attempt to keep my client and his $10,000. Too late. Discounts are not really what customers want; they want you to live your values, practice your values, and ensure everyone who works for you does the same. Values before there is a problem not after. You see with my client, it was too late, and the trust was broken. And yes, my client got their money back and went with a new developer.*

Did the first web developer do anything wrong? No, technically he did not do anything wrong. However, I would argue as a company wanting to win in the Trust & Value Economy, he lost the business because he did not deliver on his brand promise. Whether that was up to him or his team to deliver on their values, he is, as the owner, ultimately responsible.

How to know you are delivering

1. Ask your customers. Inquire about their experience, and what else could you be doing to make this a better experience.

2. Make sure you listen to the customer and are solving the right problem. Clarify with your client.

3. Communicate and be proactive. Follow-up and communication are NOT the responsibility of your customer they are yours. This is an important rule for not only you as the owner to remember, but for everyone on your team to know and understand.

4. Check your customer touch points and make sure they are positive, consistent, and are customer focused. Know what it feels like to do business with you.

5. Find opportunity to add value beyond your product or service. Make an introduction to someone they want or need to meet,

suggest a great networking opportunity for them, or give them a book or DVD that would help them with a particular challenge they are having.

Always remember your customers have a choice and a voice.

Build a foundation; build trust

In the same way that a building needs a solid foundation in order to support its structure, your business needs a firm foundation to support continued success.

Today's customers are looking to enter into a long-term relationship with you, and they need to know that your company's policies will be the same today, tomorrow, and into the future. As I have said before, consumers today are a cynical bunch with good reason to be. Actions that are inconsistent with words make consumers want to pull back. The mission and the values you so clearly place on your website need to be reflected in your daily actions.

Building trust with customers is a lot like building a savings account. In order for the trust to grow, you must make deposits into the account each time the customer encounters you. If you make enough deposits, the customer, like your savings account, grows and develops. Again, customers are sceptical, so yes, it is more difficult to instill loyalty in your customer base than it has ever been before. It is not enough to show them your values once. You must live your values, and they must witness and feel those values every time they use your services. Trust is built when, and only when, your customers eventually believe you are consistent and they can count on you, when they believe that each and every interaction with you will meet or exceed their expectations.

For example: We have this great little town center not ten minutes from our home. The area is filled with shops and restaurants. Two of the restaurants are a little more upscale and are a nice change if you are looking to get away from the flip-flops and t-shirt crowd. We consistently eat at one of the restaurants and rarely if ever darken the door of the other.

Why? The first restaurant has been consistent from the start. Since we began going there four years ago, the food has been fantastic, the service great and the atmosphere top drawer. The other, we have not eaten in since it opened three and half years ago. Our first dinner there was fantastic. However, our second was not so great. When we decided to give it one more shot, the food was excellent but the service was exceptionally bad. In addition, and probably with more impact, we heard the same reports from other friends about this restaurant. With so many places to eat, why bother to frequent a place you can't "trust" to be good, or that does not provide food and service that is worth the price you pay for it (value)?

To create trust in your prospects (make deposits into the bank account), demonstrate and take full responsibility for your business being trustworthy. This idea is the very foundation for everything you and your employees do when dealing with suppliers, customers and each other. If everyone on your team is on the same page from the very beginning, it will be much easier to carry this idea forward and build a firm foundation for your business in the new economy.

There are a number of ways that you can begin to make deposits into you customers' bank accounts, many we have covered. As previously discussed, you can let the consumer set the pace of the relationship. Instead of trying to move the selling relationship along to pressure buyers to make a decision quickly, you can adjust your business model to bend to the modern sales cycle; a sales cycle that is much more erratic and externally impacted than in the past. You can invest time, energy and knowledge really getting to know your customers, their business, their industry challenges and opportunities and then you can use this information to uncover and recommend solutions, ideas that can help them overcome the problems they are facing.

Just be yourself—and know who that is

Another way is to set yourself up to be remembered. In an overcrowded economy, where options abound and information is plentiful, you want to stand out and you want to be memorable. You have to get above the white noise, so that when customers are ready to buy you are the first person they gravitate to, the first person they think about. Again, consumers are overwhelmed. What they want is someone they enjoy and trust to do business with. They want you to make the choice easy for them. Consumers are not only confronted with an unbelievable number of places and ways to buy products and services, they are also overwhelmed with the number of sales people and business owners trying to sell to them.

So if you want to stand out from your competition, if you want to be the person consumers choose do business with then you need to be memorable. You need to not only sell a great product or service, you need to be the type of person they look forward to doing business with. Ask yourself what makes you different, what makes you stand out? Why have people turned to you for help or assistance in the past? Why have people bought from you in the past? Why did your repeat buyers come back? Why did your customers choose you over the competition?

There was a time when entrepreneurs could get rich quickly, but believe me that time is long gone. Now, you need to prepare and train for a marathon not a sprint. You need a solid foundation that is built to last for years to come, and one that can weather any storm. In the same way that trust is built by making small deposits during every consumer encounter, success will come as the result of taking the baby steps required to develop long-term relationships with your customers.

Think of success as being a product of trust, that the very path to profitability runs right through and is dependent on the relationship you build with the customer. Only when they feel trust will potential customers feel comfortable enough to buy from you.

This economy is made for anyone who is passionate about what they do, the business they promote, or the service they offer. This is a Trust & Value Economy—an economy that has consumers desperately looking for, and seeking out, services they trust, products that have value, and people with whom they can connect.

In fact, this economy is all about connection—emotional connection. So the better you know yourself and define your business, the easier it will be for you to find the right customers and build a mutually beneficial relationship with them.

KEY TAKEAWAY

To win and succeed in the Trust and Value Economy, build a strong foundation. Define your mission and your values. Then ensure every action, every process and every employee in your business aligns with those values.

CHAPTER 10

Market Your Values

In reality you and your business are unique. In the entire history of the world, there has never been a professional exactly like you or a company that operates precisely like yours. Unfortunately, however, while that may be true, our businesses look a lot like snowflakes to the average consumer. Each one may be unique, but from the view of the person watching the snowfall, the flakes look exactly the same. Your job is to get your customer interested enough to see what makes you different.

Wow!

Getting customers to know and understand what makes you different plays an important role in winning in the Trust & Value Economy. It takes a "wow" factor. Something that not only makes you stand out from your competition but makes you stand out period! What makes you unique and different is already there; you just need to uncover it, clearly define it and then share it.

Often in business we call this "wow" our brand, and for the sake of simplicity I am going to use that term. However, the term "brand," like so many other words in our culture, has been "watered" down from overuse and misuse. I want you to think of your "brand" as how you and your company are viewed in totality by the rest of the world.

You want to create a brand, a reputation, a "wow" so distinctive that it transcends what your business sells and offers. A "wow" factor is just that "wow!" People have heard of you, and they like what they've heard. So much so that when you come calling, they want to meet you. And the opportunity to do business with your company is something they would consider a lucky opportunity.

That is what you are going for, that is the type of brand you want to build. You want doors to open before you even knock on them, or better yet to have the customer come knocking on your door.

You know the truth is we never really quite get past high school. We all want to be in the popular crowd and run with the "in" group. Business is no different; your goal is to be the "popular" choice, the one that everyone wants to work with, the star everyone wants to be around. Well, there is one thing different about business. In high school, we excluded people. In business, you want to build a customer base that includes and makes everyone feel welcome. Even if you do not necessarily want to do business with them, you still want to be approachable, kind, and to be a business of which they speak highly.

Take a minute right now to think about your brand and put yourself in your customer's shoes. Ask yourself:

Question 1: Would you buy something from you and your company?

If the answer is anything less than a resounding "Yes," you have some work to do on your brand and your company.

Question 2: Why would you buy something from you over one of your competitors?

If you cannot quickly and concisely answer that question then you have some work to do on your unique identity.

I want to emphasize the phrase "quickly and concisely" as the gauge as to whether you have identified and engaged with your own unique identity. You have to feel your brand. You have to be emotionally connected to it before you can even begin to hope that it resonates with your customers. If you ever hope to get the customer to buy into your brand, you must be bought in first. And your answers to those two questions are a good place to start your evaluation of how to develop the distinctive appeal of your brand. If you cannot give a whole-hearted endorsement of your brand, consider what makes you less than enthusiastic. Ask yourself:

Questions 1: What would make you want to buy not only your product but also to buy it from you?

Questions 2: What is so appealing about what you offer and how you offer it?

Once you answer the questions, you can move on to figuring out how to share that message with the world. Okay maybe not the world, just yet, but with your current customer base and your future customer base...and then the world.

You will know you have succeeded in building a successful brand when people are talking about you, recommending you, and you become the "go to" person for whatever product or service you represent.

I was with a client of mine, a marketing specialist, and as we were wrapping things up, her cell phone rang with a number she did not recognize, so she let it go to voicemail. As we walked to our cars, she played the message, smiled and asked me to listen to it. It was a gentleman who was asking for a meeting. He said he was new to town and had asked around about who to talk with regarding marketing. Her name had come up three times, in three different conversations, so he knew she was the one to talk with. That is creating a "unique" identity. Our community has a marketing specialist on every corner, yet my client and her company stand out.

Clearly defining the unique aspects of your business gives prospects a reason to choose you, and gives your existing customers a reason to stay with you when the competition comes calling.

My investment banker is a great example of someone with a "wow" factor. My husband and I have been with him for years. We've had plenty of other investment bankers come and ask for our business—investment advisors that use those creative and unique sales lines like "let me just give you a second opinion," or "this is just a simple review" or "I can give you some ideas on where to ask for more from your current investment advisor." Believe me they are good! However, I always say "No thank you, we are happy." Why? Because our investment banker has invested the time and energy in creating his "wow" factor, his own unique identity.

Let me tell you about him. For the last five years, our investment advisor has placed top five in his company, a financial firm that was rated one of the top 100 most safe and sound in the country. In addition, whenever his name comes up at cocktail parties and on the golf course, people just can't say enough good things about his work and his leadership in our community.

Now, it sounds like I know an awful lot about him, doesn't it? Well, I don't know these things about my investment advisor because I am some crazed woman who is obsessed with her investment advisor; I know these things because he is outstanding at creating his own "wow" factor. When he finishes top five in his company, he sends us a note thanking us for being his clients and helping him achieve this level of success. When the financial institution was named in the Top 100 Most Safe and Sound, he sent us a copy of the article, with a note just wanting us to know that we are in good hands. And since he does this with all of his clients, we all naturally talk about it when we are at an event, at a cocktail party or are on the golf course. He gives us a reason to be proud of his success, to be associated with him, to talk about him. Yes, he has created his "wow" factor.

In the Trust & Value Economy, consumers are looking for a way to narrow their options, to make their choices easier, and they do this by finding something they recognize, something they have heard of, and someone they are familiar with. Consumers today are attracted to, and more willing to do business with, companies that foster a sense of familiarity that breeds confidence with prospects and customers alike. It is the beginning of an emotional connection.

True "wow" comes from within

Neither your identity nor your business' identity should be dictated by fluctuating trends among your competitors or what you think will fill a void in the existing market. Your identity, your brand, your "wow" factor is not external—it is internal.

Changing with each passing trend makes you stand out less in a business world saturated with competition and fads. It also creates a sense of instability for your existing customer base. In a consumer culture where trendy products become obsolete as quickly as social media status updates, many consumers crave stable and familiar professionals and establishments. Instead of looking for marketing gimmicks, spend some time thinking about what gives you and your company unique and lasting appeal.

Authenticity is key in establishing a successful professional and business "wow" factor. True "wow," lasting "wow," isn't about hype and posturing. Your customers will ultimately see through even the most suave marketing strategy. A far better choice is to invest the time to create a reliable brand that builds your reputation and one that ensures consistency and quality for your customer/client base. Today's frugal buyers want to know, before they buy, what they will get every time they deal with you and your company, especially if they can get a similar product or service elsewhere.

Get back to the basics

Your company can't possibly be all things to all potential buyers—and that's where you start to build your brand. You begin this process by getting to know yourself and your company. What is unique, different and appealing about you? When you are trying to sculpt your "wow," find out what qualities most appeal and are most important to your best customers. Make it simple. Ask your valued clients and customers:

- Why do you do business with us?

- Why are you willing to pay more for our product or service?

- What keeps you coming back?

What you'll find (or should find) is their answers align squarely and cleanly with your corporate values and the reputation you have been working to build.

Keep in mind that a brand doesn't exist to statically represent your company—it is a consistent way of reminding your customers what you stand for and what value you offer. It works in conjunction with your values, and it attracts attention and plants a seed. A great brand is simple and descriptive enough to grow with you.

Here are some great examples of what other companies do and where they focus:

- *The experience you create for your customer*—High Point University

- *The way you stand behind your product*—LL Bean

- *The ease of using your product; the support you provide*—Apple

- *The innovation and creativity of your company*—Google

- *The dedication to spoiling your customers*—Ritz Carlton

- *The commitment to low cost*—Walmart

Be sure to consider your market carefully before you decide which areas to emphasize and how to define your brand. Focusing on your discount prices and extra offers with a purchase may actually be a turnoff to consumers if you are running a niche market boutique for imported Italian business suits. The success or failure of a new business often depends on making a good first impression on customers. Taking the time to do a bit of extra research into the values that appeal to your target audience will enable you to carefully craft an idea of your brand that permeates your customers' experience before they ever walk through your door.

The best company brands are the simple ones. The average consumer is exposed to so much noise on a daily basis, your customers and clients don't need more. They need something that rings true, something they can rely on, rather than something that's trying to manipulate them and further complicate their decision-making process. When you create a branding statement use as few words as possible to get your point across. You want it clean—so your customer just gets it. What will your customers get from you that they cannot get anywhere else?

Looks matter

Once you have decided which aspects of the business you are going to focus on for branding purposes, make sure that this concept is included in every aspect of your business, from your marketing materials, to your sales approach, to your delivery.

In order for a brand to stand out, it must present a consistent, appealing message to your potential client base that builds trust and value. For a brand to really do its work, it must be present in much more than the cool marketing materials and great logo. A brand is a way you make a customer feel, a promise that you make, and one on which you deliver. A brand, your unique identity, is reflected in the experience your customer has.

That said, when it comes to brand, your logo and colors do matter. When it comes to brand, truly everything matters. The designs you use need to reflect the emotion you are trying to convey.

I have a client, a hospital, that prides itself on being home to physicians offering the most advanced procedures with the most high-tech surgical equipment available. When we reviewed their brand, we found a logo designed in 1984. Their colors were blue and gold. The entire look was dated. If there was one message that logo and those colors conveyed it was that this hospital was old and behind the times. This was a small but very important element that needed to change if they were going to deliver on their brand.

Believe it or not, colors say a lot to the consumer. They often even have cultural associations. Take the time to find out which tones best convey the impression you want to leave on consumers. For example, if you want to send a message that your business is part of the green industry movement or has adopted environmentally-friendly

133

policies, make sure that you incorporate emerald or olive tones into your website, brochures, letterhead and other promotional items. Financial organizations will also want to use green in their branding efforts, but as a way to indicate money and wealth. If you are trying to promote a dating site, you probably want to use red to symbolize love and passion as part of your corporate brand. Strike a balance between main colors and accents that reflect which issues are most important to your company. The colors and images you choose will be ones your customers will associate with your business, so make sure that all of them complement your brand.

Is taking the time to choose just the right color and logo for your business worth the effort? Seems silly doesn't it? A brand delivers a series of subtle messages that need to align, speak with one voice and convey one message. When one part of your brand is off, yes even your colors and your logo, you send the signal of uncertainty to anyone encountering your brand. Brand *is* that sensitive and that powerful.

No violation of brand sensitivity makes me crazier these days than hospitals. They all, pretty much every single one, are trying to position themselves as healthcare leaders in their community. Hospitals all over the country are trying to get out on the preventative side of the healthcare crisis, engaging in health fairs, nutrition and exercise programs, and pushing us all to take personal responsibility for our health.

Well have you been to the hospital lately? For the most part they are the antithesis of good health. First their cafeterias are filled with bad food choices. Bad food choices, can you believe it, at the hospital? In addition, the poor patients in the room recovering from surgery or illness, do not stand a chance with what is sent to their room.

Pancakes, syrup, grits and bacon for breakfast or fried chicken and cake for dinner? Who eats like that, let alone why do organizations that are positioning themselves, branding themselves as health leaders, even have that as an option?

Now let's talk about the staff. First let me say I cannot stress enough that being a nurse or a doctor today is one of the most demanding jobs that there is and it is pressure filled. So with that said, I still want to question the brand of an organization that claims to be health conscious but does little to encourage and support the weight challenges, smoking issues, and nutritional challenges of their staff. Hospitals, or any companies that hope to brand themselves as a resource and a leader for health, need to take a strong, internal look at what their organization and their team are conveying, day in and day out, about their message.

You are your brand

By establishing your brand, you give your customers information up front. You let them know all about you and about your business and what it can do for them. A brand is what a consumer thinks, what emotional connection they have when they hear the name of your business. Your brand is your reputation—and it is an indicator of the level of trust you have engendered from your customers.

When a customer or client decides to buy from your business, they are choosing to buy from you. Never forget that. This has never been more true than in this economy. Consumers today have no expectation that a company will be here five years from now, ten years from now. Constant bank mergers, closings and the fall of long-time established companies changed everything in this country. As

135

consumers, we no longer look to establish a long-term relationship with a company; we look to establish a long-term relationship with a person. In today's economy, we have far more faith a person will be here in five years, then we do a company will be.

Whether or not a customer has confidence in the product you provide is a direct reflection on his view of your integrity and commitment to quality. You can choose to build your brand around any number of concepts, as long as they accurately reflect the values and standards of you and your company. Identify what makes your company, products and services worthwhile to a potential client, why they should care, and then create a consistent, authentic brand that customers can trust.

Thus, the commitment to creating a brand must extend to each and every member of your team. If your company brand and the individuals representing that brand do not embrace, embody and speak the same language, then your unique identity, your brand, will fall flat and lose its power.

Your brand builds your community

A brand is not a direct source of profit, but it is an extremely important source of intangible value. A brand that accurately reflects your reputation and that of your company will build consistency with your customers. And consistency leads to trust. Once customers or clients have responded to your brand by choosing your company as the right one for them, they will reward you with repeat business and refer other people to you. (Creating the perfect opportunity for you to focus firmly on what else you can do to further enhance and solidify your reputation and your brand with your loyal customers.)

The goal in creating your unique identity is to create an idea around your business that makes customers want—no wait!—*have* to choose to do business with you time and again. You are not looking to make a single sale and move on to the next buyer. That type of strategy is not going to foster long-term loyalty or success in the Trust & Value Economy. Remember happy customers are repeat customers, and repeat customers become referring customers and advocates.

Customers who are attracted to your reputation and ultimately are loyal to your brand will be essential players in your ability to innovate, adapt and change. A successful brand creates a community of tried-and-true supporters who can be counted on to suggest improvements, point out mistakes, and help you test or try out changes until you land on the best one. A strong brand builds a customer base that wants you to win, and roots for you to succeed, and is willing to help you get there. Unlike a consumer who isn't engaged with your brand, these consumers don't need your offerings to be perfect to have anything to do with you. They have bought in, and they aren't likely to give up on you over a misstep—instead, they'll act as partners to help your company be the best it can be.

Taking the time to consider exactly what makes you and your company worth a consumer's trust and to create your own "wow" factor means your consistent brand is a major key to success in the Trust & Value Economy. A recognizable name with a reputation for quality will ensure you jump off the shelf and give consumers a reason to choose you. In addition, it will give your business far greater longevity than even the best marketing campaigns. This initial extra effort will not only set your business apart from the transient, trendy businesses that consumers learn to avoid, but will also foster long-term loyalty from your customer/client base.

KEY TAKEAWAY

To win in the Trust & Value Economy, put the time and energy into developing, building and delivering your brand. Understand that brand is an outreach of your overall growth and business development strategy.

CHAPTER 11

Relationship Building 101

S am Erwin and Lee Dixon, CEO and COO respectively of the
Palmetto Bank, took over their bank at its darkest hour.

*Where most in the business community saw insurmountable
odds, Sam and Lee saw opportunity and a chance to rise to the
challenge and reinvent their bank. (And in my opinion, what they
have done will greatly influence the future of the banking industry;
an industry that I think we can all agree desperately needs an
overhaul.) The story of where they have been and where they are
now is nothing short of inspiring.*

*One has only to look at the bank's makeover and resurgence to
realize that one thing that is always at the front of the minds of
these two executives is strengthening the client experience. The
question they ask themselves daily, the challenge they bring to their
team on a continual basis, and the subject that they will never
allow to be removed from everyday conversations and strategy
sessions is how to build a bank, a team and an overall culture
that consistently increase the value of the franchise by continually
enhancing the client experience.*

On a daily basis, you'll find the leaders of the Palmetto Bank meeting and strategizing, not just about budgets, stock prices and their bottom line, but primarily on how to enhance the client experience. They call this a Value Creation Strategy. They invest their time questioning and testing their current value to their clients, challenging their team on how to improve it, and holding themselves accountable to place client perspective at the center of their plan to build a sound and profitable financial institution.

The idea—which, yes, screams integrity, ethics and morality—does so much more. Both Sam and Lee will be the first to tell you that it also screams profitability. They firmly believe that profitability is an outcome of their strategy.

Both of these visionaries understand that in the Trust & Value Economy, the only way to find growth, build your bottom line, and continue to attract the best team talent is to make the client the heart of your business strategy. Once you achieve success in this arena, continue to question and challenge yourself on the level of value, you are adding to the existing relationship and what you need to add to stay ahead of the competition. Sam and Lee understand that this is a goal that is never really reached.

This is relationship building at its finest, because relationships begin with value. There are many steps involved in building a healthy business that cannot be accomplished all in one day. Companies that try to rush the relationship-building process are going to find that they are not seeing sustained long-term growth.

If you choose to patiently invest the necessary time and energy to build credibility with prospective customers, you will find that long-term loyalty is a positive aspect that the Trust & Value Economy holds for you; it is an aspect with a high rate of return.

Relationships take time

Good relationships don't happen overnight. We know from our own life experience. We all can appreciate how uncomfortable we'd feel if a person we'd only been dating a week insisted on knowing whether or not we were ready to get married. Even if we were interested in getting to know the person better, the pressure to close the deal quickly would make that person seem far less appealing.

The best relationships, whether personal or professional, take time to develop. Your ideal customers are out there waiting to be won, but you will have to court them first. Your best strategy is patience combined with a complete focus on them as your customer.

Your patience shows that you respect your customers enough to give them the time they need to make a decision about if and when to buy from you. If you present yourself and what your company has to offer honestly and with respect for their needs, your prospective customers will appreciate the positive atmosphere you create and be much more likely to go with your company when they are ready to make their purchase.

Relationships are built on understanding

When is the last time you walked through your company as a customer? Great question, right?

Your answer should be not be less than three months ago. When we work for a company and handle the day-to-day operations, the way we see what goes on there is very different from what our customer sees. Customers have an entirely different perspective of our company than we do.

So if we are going to build our relationship with them and improve their experience, we need to take time and get inside their heads and minds. We need to see our business from the customer's perspective.

In the Trust & Value Economy, this is critical. You need to know not only what they experience, but what it looks like and feels like to be your customer. Is it good? Bad? Exceptional? Or just okay? Walking in their shoes will provide the perspective you need and let you know exactly what to do to push your business to the next level.

As we've discussed, what you are selling is a commodity. How you sell it is your competitive advantage. Building a relationship means customer care. And customer care is about being reactive to their needs and wants. To create an exceptional customer be proactive and dedicate yourself to looking for opportunities to identify your customers' needs before they do. Find innovative and creative ways to exceed their expectations and, well frankly, just blow their minds.

Creating the customer experience

So how do create an experience, exceed expectations, and uncover what your customers really want? After you've walked in their shoes and gained insights from that, take your inquiry a bit deeper. Talk to your customers. If you ever hope to exceed customer expectations, you need to understand their current expectations of you, your product and your company.

One thing I can guarantee is that customers who are satisfied are not going to voluntarily take time out of their already jam-packed schedule to let you know how you're doing. Those who are not happy will simply go find one of your competitors who they believe is better able to meet their needs.

Discovering the impression your company is making on consumers requires a deliberate effort on your part. How do you determine how well your company is doing? Discover where you fall on the customer experience ladder? Again, begin by asking your customers.

True wisdom I know. It is not just enough to ask and get the words back, you need more.

As human beings, we don't like confrontation or rejection. We don't like telling people something they may not want to hear or even make a suggestion that we fear will not be accepted. How many times do you get a customer survey or someone asks you how your experience was and you simply say, "Fine, thank you"?

So just like everything else in this book and in this economy, how you ask people needs to be on steroids, ramped up and done on a deeper and much larger scale. Because, unless a bond is built, unless we trust that the person asking really wants to hear the answer, we will never share the information the person is truly looking for.

The way to successfully learn what your customers need is by getting to know them. Asking what they need, and finding out more about the when, where, and why behind their purchases. It is amazing how easy it can be to overlook this measure. As business owners and entrepreneurs, we tend to be passionate about our idea and its successful execution. It is easy to get so caught up in all the improvements and plans we've dreamed up that we forget to ask the very reason for our business—our customers—how our product or service can become as indispensable to them as oxygen.

There are three ways that I suggest finding out how your company is doing: one-on-one meetings, focus groups and surveys. There is a lot of debate as to which avenue is the best, but I believe for solid results you need to combine all three. And that is taking your "asking" to an entirely new level. Each one has its advantages and disadvantages. So the combination of the three will give you just the information you need to continuously and consistently enhance the customer experience and build your relationship. A commitment at this level on your part also sends a strong message to the customer that you are really interested, you really care and you really want to know. That furthers that bond of trust.

What to ask and how to ask it

Before you begin, decide what you want to know and design your process for how you will ask. Take the time to work with your peers or your team and design a short set of open-ended questions that will uncover the type of information you would like to know: What is working for them? What is not? And What would they like to see changed?

Many experts advocate offering some sort of incentive (a discount, a gift card, etc.) for answering survey questions. I do not. I think people, especially your customers, want to help you and want you to do well, so they will answer your questions without incentive. If you want to thank specific customers then do that separately and in a way that is unique and holds value for them.

Let's take a look at the three ways to engage your customers in feedback.

1. **One-on-one interviews**—This is my personal favorite because I get to spend quality time with a customer, show them how truly interested I am, and have the opportunity to allow the conversation to go many different directions.

How do you get started? Well it is pretty easy. Just make a list of the customers you would like to hear from and you feel would give you honest feedback. Then simply pick up the phone and ask them to coffee, to lunch or for a few moments of their time next time they are in your facility. Approach people with a simple, "I would love your input and advice;" "We are trying to enhance our customer's experience," or "It would be a great help if you could answer a few questions."

Yes, hard to believe but it is that easy to get started. Oh, and make sure you include that, while you appreciate any positive feedback, the goal is to improve the experience to get better. This gives them permission to give you negative feedback or suggestions on how to take the experience to an entirely new level.

If this is not something you want to do yourself, you can engage a company or an intern with a local college (under the direction of his/her professor) to do a formal interview process for you. I have done them both ways and got great results. You simply design questions, create a list of customers to be contacted, and let those customers know (preferably with a personal note or call from you) that you have engaged this independent party to help you improve your service. Then let everyone else take it from there.

2. **Focus Groups**—Focus groups are a great tool. Get a group of customers (about eight to ten) in a room, ask them questions, and let them discuss what is working for them, what is not, and how it can improve. What I love about focus groups is the brainstorming aspect and the body language. It is amazing how many times the words out of their mouths say one thing and their actions or facial expressions reveal another. Focus groups truly give you the opportunity to listen and observe.

145

In addition, by getting customers together you give them the opportunity to feed off one another, and you generally get some innovative and very creative feedback. Again, you can do focus groups yourself or hire an outside facilitator to do them for you. A professional facilitator can create an atmosphere that yields stronger results, but if budget concerns are an issue, do not hesitate to do this yourself or, again, engage a college student and the support of his/her professor. The important step is that you hold the focus group; a professional facilitator is a bonus.

3. **The Survey**—A very simple way for you to keep a finger on the pulse of your customers' thinking is to invite them to participate in a short customer satisfaction survey. If you are seeing customers at a brick and mortar location, invite them to fill out a brief survey on the spot. You are more likely to get a higher number of respondents if you have the customer share his or her thoughts right away. If you don't have that luxury, I have a number of clients that do online surveys. Online surveys work great, as all respondents have to do is hit reply to send them on to you.

   Keep your survey (in fact, keep all of these feedback tools) short and to the point. Overwhelming customers with a long list of questions can accomplish the opposite of your intention, which was demonstrating your commitment to their needs. If you make the survey too long, your customers will be less likely to take the time to fill it out or will leave feeling annoyed with your company. Use this as an opportunity to see how well you are delivering the values promised in your marketing and branding campaign. Make sure that your questions are simple, pointed and relevant. Rating scales or multiple choice are the best options for surveys.

To maximize the effectiveness of customer feedback in surveys, leave a space where customers can write in comments if they wish. This space gives them the opportunity to share not only the things they like about your business, products and services but also any concerns or complaints.

Again, I like using a combination of all three tools in my customer feedback strategy. People communicate differently and feel comfortable in different ways, so providing options ensures you touch your customers and get varying levels of feedback.

Use What You Learn

Now, there are two more critical steps in customer feedback.

Step 1: You need to use the feedback.

Step 2: You need to communicate to those who participated what the results were and how you are going to use them.

Pay careful attention here. One of the worst things you can do is ask customers for their opinion and then ignore those opinions. Even if you are not in a position to implement their ideas right away, thank them for their feedback, let them know you heard them, validate their feelings, and share your plan of action, whatever it is, big or small.

Again, your customers want to help you, and when you ask for their opinion, share the results and then take action. You have just moved customer experience and your relationship to a whole new level.

Customer feedback—asking for it and acting on it—is actually a great additional marketing tool. Great customers want to "belong" to your business, feel a part of it, and asking and using their feedback is a great way to do that.

Getting customer feedback should not be a side note in your plans. Do not chase new business until you understand and have secured your existing business. You do not need any new customers if you are not effectively serving (and you do not effectively understand) the customers you already have.

If you can identify your best customers and why they do business with you, and have educated your team on this, your business is ready to grow. If not, you need to invest some time and resources in learning more about your current base before expanding.

I have a client who has a "client thank you wall." My client routinely engages in customer feedback, and has done so for years because he gains so many terrific ideas from it. About five years ago, he purchased one of those large screen televisions for his lobby. You have seen those televisions that give you information and updates about the company while you are standing there waiting for your appointment. My client, in his infinite wisdom, decided to use the television "wall," as he calls it, to both share information about his company and also to thank his clients (with their permission of course) for their ideas. This is brilliant, just brilliant. It both cements his relationship with his clients, makes them feel special, and it consistently and continually tells his other clients just how dedicated and committed he is to improving their experiences.

Buying is a relationship—and relationship are emotional

Let's go back to that first date. On first dates, we look nice, smell nice; we behave politely. We take our date to a nice restaurant. We want

148

our date to enjoy himself or herself. We want to make our date laugh. We want them to feel good, to begin to trust us. Basically, we build a "customer experience" to build a relationship.

When our customers hand us their hard-earned money, they are doing more than entering into a financial transaction, they are trusting us to follow through on what we've promised. And they are basing that trust on the quality of the relationship we've built. And that's emotional.

In a Trust & Value Economy, where our customers can buy our products and services anywhere, emotion definitely reigns supreme. To emotionally connect with your customers, you have to build trust and value—put your effort into getting to know them the way you would start any long-term relationship.

Buying has always been emotional. Kids understand this, and are masters of the art of selling via emotion. Think of the Girl Scout selling cookies or the young kid asking to mow your lawn. Kids get it. They invest first in hooking our emotions, then on selling the product.

My husband and I, along with some ambitious friends, were out for a 40-mile cycling ride one Saturday. As we came within the last three miles, we crossed paths with two blonde, freckle-faced young girls selling lemonade. Now, I love a lemonade stand. The young girls behind the operation were so proud, eager, and shameless about their promotion that we pulled our bikes to a halt immediately to buy a glass. I mean who doesn't want to support that kind of endeavor, right?

As we approached, I noticed that the "for sale" sign said $1.00 (yes, the prices have gone up). We gladly ordered some, thanked *the kids and gave them a short pep talk reinforcing how great it was they were out there, working hard and providing lemonade to thirsty riders. I asked them how much money they had made, and the little girl looked at me and said, "A lot. People just keep giving us extra money, and no one wants any money back. They must really like it." Meaning the lemonade.*

We got the biggest laugh out of that. I mean honestly, ask yourself was the lemonade so delicious that people just felt compelled to pay extra for it? I don't think so! Ever had lemonade made by two little kids in your neighborhood? Not too good, right?

The reality is the product was just a sideshow. It was the emotional feel that the passersby (consumer) had for the business and the business owners (the kids) that made people want to pay for it. In short, it was more than the product that made people want to buy their lemonade there; it was the emotional connection and the experience.

Sure, it was offered at the right time—in hot weather, in a place where people didn't have a lot of other options for a cold beverage. But it wasn't something anyone of them just had to have or, let's face it, probably even wanted.

The truth is the customers of the lemonade stand saw value in the business itself. They wanted to support the proprietors, wanted to contribute to the cause. It made them part of a community and in turn gave them a feeling of satisfaction. These customers were emotionally engaged and connected.

If you want to know how to compete in this economy, take a lesson from these kids and the lemonade stand. Try to give people the same sensation that buying from a lemonade stand does. You need to be selling more than your product, you need to selling and conveying an experience, an emotion in the sales process. Your product or service has to be a good offer. (I doubt that an offering of soup would have done quite as well on a hot summer day.) But a great product will only get you so far. Your transaction needs to ooze experience and emotion as well as value.

And emotion and experience have everything to do with service, meeting the individual needs of your customers and cementing your relationship. Even if your business is not strictly involved in the service industry, understand that in this economy you are part of the customer service industry. Customers have higher expectations in the Trust & Value Economy. They expect a company to earn their business and their continuing loyalty. In this economy, sales begin and end with service to the customer. It's important for you as a business owner and a sales professional to be thinking of how you can bring value to your customers and continue to build your relationship.

KEY TAKEAWAY

To win in the Trust & Value Economy, build your relationship with your customers by enhancing the customer experience. The best way to enhance it is to gain an understanding of your customers and how they see your business.

CHAPTER 12

Connections are the New Currency

T hink about the professionals you hire, the vendors you use and
who you work with on a regular basis—how many of them
did you call up after seeing an ad in the phone book or conducting a
random online search? Probably none, right.

This is the Trust & Value Economy. Who you know is as important, if not more important, than what you know. In this economy relationships and being connected are everything. In a world that is becoming increasingly disconnected, connections are the new currency, the very thing that research shows we most crave.

All things being equal—skills, talent, education—the more people you know, the more people you help, the more successful you will be. Not only will you have more friends and more fun, but you will, on the average, make more money, get more promotions and get more "lucky" breaks.

In this economy, connections are everything. An interesting fact is that in life just 15 percent of our success is due to our technical skill, 85 percent is due to our ability to get along and connect with people. We spend our entire lives building and developing our technical skills, but little to none to improving our ability to connect. Yet connection is where the value is, connection is your great opportunity for growth in the trust and value economy.

Reap what you sow

That's why in a Trust & Value Economy who you know is just as important as what you know. The lone wolf who operates as a one-man (or one-woman) show is finished. And we shouldn't be sad to see them go—those operating modes don't foster trust in relationships with others.

Relationships must include elements of give and take if they are going to be successful. A standoffish approach does not jive well with the current economic climate. Buying is emotional after all.

Instead, you need to actively cultivate relationships on a continuous basis. The more people you know, the more people you will be able to help through your business. If you maintain this open and sharing attitude, you will naturally attract people who will be able to help you reach your goals. This is a classic example of reaping what you sow in business. And it's as true today as when that saying was first uttered.

In order for people to feel comfortable doing business with you, they have to feel that they know you. If you have done the work involved in developing a large network of contacts, growing your business is going to be a much easier (and more enjoyable) process. In this new economy, your business success will depend on how well you are able to develop positive relationships with others.

Through building connections, you can avoid the stress, anxiety and struggle of blatantly chasing business. Imagine that—giving up the constant stress of chasing business. Instead, you get to focus on discovering how you can better service your existing customers, prospective buyers, suppliers, and anyone else in your circle of acquaintances. Done effectively, this will put you in a position to attract business to your organization that stems purely from the relationships you have developed and continue to develop with people.

This approach has such appealing simplicity. Don't think of yourself as a hunter, aggressively pursuing sales, but as a relationship builder, determinedly finding solutions for your contacts.

The hunter mentality implies that you pursue revenue generation activities only during certain designated times. Whereas, if you sustain a network of people you interact with regularly, sales activity will occur naturally and without pressure. A culture and an environment built on connections is one that is healthier for you, your customers and for your sales team.

It also has staying power. Rather than focusing only on a short-term result (making a sale), you can build a business that benefits from long-term relationships with a group of people who will come to you time and time again for their needs—without you having to "sell" them on what you have to offer.

Combine your ability to build connections with your ability to choose qualified prospects, and you have an unbeatable combination. After all, we know that people are not coming to us for the product—they can get that anywhere; they are coming for the experience and for what they believe they will get from us.

Take a cue from grandpa

This is not a new concept, just a steadfast and true concept ramped up and pushed into high gear. According to Gary Vaynerchuck, author of *Crush It* and *The Thank You Economy*, our grandparents are actually better prepared to succeed in this economy then we are. Wow! Why? Because our grandparents did business in a time when success was determined by building relationships and making connections.

Our grandparents understood that the product or service was just the beginning; the ability to connect with customers and build long-term relationships was where the business was built and how it would grow. We have only to look to our grandparents' lives. They wrote the book on how to engage, build trust and add value. Now it is time for us to get it out, dust it off and start reading.

It may sound counterintuitive given all the technology and quick fix expectations we have today. But it's true. Our grandparents were only successful in business if they were successful in building relationships and making connections. It was truly non-negotiable in their time. They operated in an environment where engaging, building trust and adding value were key. In their case, it was not technology that enabled their consumer to go elsewhere—word-of-mouth communication and peer recommendations constituted the majority of their "marketing." Without relationships, they didn't have a prayer of finding customers.

For our grandparents, it might have seemed silly to even have a term for "networking." It wasn't a separate effort. It was part and parcel of running a business. Today we hear the term networking and often think of it as something we must do to get ahead. It elicits grimaces and starts headaches—it feels selfish and impersonal. I believe that the more people you know, the more opportunities you will have to impact them in a way that eventually improves your sales process.

Network naturally

Be careful though. Just as many of the traditional sales techniques are outdated, so are many of the networking skills you have been taught. I do not endorse many of the robotic techniques suggested and employed to beef up contact lists and make people think you're taking an interest in them. The key is not so much technique as intention—if you intend to get to know someone and you are genuinely interested in what makes them tick, you will see your connections naturally skyrocket. Be authentic in your desire to learn about and invest in other people first.

157

Whenever I meet someone networking, whether online or in person (yes I network often online), I am always impressed by those who take a real interest in me. They are not trying to tell me about themselves, their companies or sell me something; they are investing in getting to know me, believing that if there is an opportunity here it will emerge. They have carefully chosen me (according to their prospect criteria list) as someone to reach out to, and allow the relationship to unfold naturally. This builds trust, and builds a willingness on my part to engage and get involved with this person.

Networking through volunteering is a great opportunity to showcase your values, your skills and the type of company you represent. When we get involved in causes we care about, lend our skills and talents to help, our customers get to try us on for size so to speak. When they volunteer with us or see the benefits of our hard volunteer hours, they have the information they need to take the next step to choose us as someone they want to do business with.

Building your network

Investing in this new currency of connections takes time. Any expectation of instant gratification is a pipe dream. But the return will be well worth the effort. This currency deals in emotions and shows its value most when people are willing to spend their treasured time with you. When they open up to you about themselves, their businesses and their families, their hobbies, and even their dreams, you know you have a golden opportunity on your hands.

But don't see it as an opportunity for you. It is an opportunity for you to help them meet a need. If you fail to see that, then networking never becomes anything greater. You can go round and round meeting new people and collecting business cards, but you'll never truly connect enough to make it count for them, for you or for your business. People who will come up winners in the Trust & Value Economy already know the value of connections.

Are you prepared to spend the time necessary to do what it takes to develop your network? Somewhere in the last decade the importance of soft skills slipped away and was replaced with assertive techniques, pushy sales and persistent follow-up. Well, luckily for both our customers and us, the arts of conversation, relationship and connection are back. They're back, and they're working.

If you want to make this new economy your economy, then take a good long look at how you currently build connections, your sales techniques, your marketing approach and your customers' experience. Ensure all of them are rooted in emotional connection, engagement, trust and value. And ensure all include these three strategies to build and enhance your network:

1. **Push don't pull**—Ask yourself: Are you pushing your customers to buy or your prospects to get to know you? Or are you pulling them to learn more about your product or service? Your business growth strategy needs to be built around your ability to pull your customers in rather than pushing them to make a decision. In a shifting economy, that has heavy competition, consumers are in control. You can do a lot to influence their decision, but since they are inundated with choices, the decision to buy remains theirs. You push you lose; you pull you gain a customer for life.

2. **Blend don't separate**—14 percent of consumers trust traditional advertising, 78 percent trust peer recommendations. To succeed in today's economy, blend, don't separate, your traditional and social-media advertising with your networking. Make people

aware of who you are and what you do via traditional channels. But also engage, connect and build trust through social networks, forums and traditional networking events and channels. Invite people to experience, share and comment about your company. Give them the ability to define and draw others into the value of your brand.

3. **Niche, don't expand**—While we all realize the economy has changed, do we really realize just how much it has changed? Consumers are different now—they want to be sure of who they are connecting with, what they are buying. They want to believe in the person they are buying from, and they want to verify and validate their choice. They are looking for experts. While our gut reaction is to offer anything to anyone willing to buy, the truth is the more we narrow our focus the more our market will expand. To be successful, define your niche, decide what you want to be known for and what clients you really want to serve. The better we niche, the better we can define our brand and the more we engage our target market to create trust and value.

Yes, the market has changed and so have the rules. This is an economy for people who wear their values on their sleeve, and who are filled with passion and caring for others. This is an economy for people willing to invest in the success of others before they worry about their own success. That is the type of individual who will be successful in this economy. And that is who you need to be in order for your customers to feel comfortable not only doing business with you but also referring potential customers to you. People have to feel that they know you.

True connection is a two-way street—the super-fan

Even more than the quality of your products or the actual need for your services, the sense that you are a trustworthy business acquaintance determines whether or not an individual will risk their own reputation to send business your way. Providing consistent, positive experiences with you and your company will increase the likelihood that a customer or business associate will refer you to people within their extended networks. Once you have done the initial work involved in developing a large network of contacts, investing in the success of others, growing your business will be a much easier (and more enjoyable) process.

With this strong connection, the relationship with your customers goes beyond a simple purchase. You, in a sense, create super-fans! Think of how little effort it takes to sell a prospect, deepen a client relationship or turn a profit when it all begins with a current client who is loyal.

This past year, I took on a new client who actually came to me via a loyal client of mine. He is the CEO of a manufacturing company, and he is passionate, to say the least, about his customers. He goes above and beyond without thinking twice about it. He is so aligned with his values that his leadership and his entire team do business on a daily business just exactly the way he does it, putting customer needs first and foremost.

When we first met to discuss how we might begin working together, he shared his story of this economic downturn and the impact it had not only on his business but also on how he now feels about the importance of his most loyal clients.

Being in manufacturing, my client felt the shift in this economy pretty hard when it hit in 2008. Three of his five biggest clients were in the business of supplying large equipment to real estate and development firms. Needless to say their business dried up almost overnight.

At first, he was frozen in fear, completely unsure of what to do or where to go. One day over lunch, he was sharing his concerns with one of his most valued clients, someone whom he had worked with for more than 20 years and someone he had done a lot to support. He had invested in both the relationship and his client's business.

After listening to the entire story, his loyal client had an idea. He suggested that my client expand into new markets and different industries. And he had just the contact to help him do that. He knew several of his peers would love to use my client as their vendor, and he would be happy not only to make the introductions but also recommend him as well.

Within six months my client had four new multimillion dollar clients. Instead of laying employees off, he was hiring. That is how we found each other. He saw such huge potential for his company that he brought me on to develop his leadership team and train his sales force. It is a truly amazing example of the power of loyal customers.

Super-fans become brand ambassadors; those who enjoy and are attracted to not only your product but their buying experience with you. They feel confident about the purchase and are less likely to stress out when researching or making a decision about the buy. They are therefore also less likely to put off the purchase or decision for later.

162

A loyal customer is a happy customer, a consistent customer and ultimately an advocate helping you build your business. Yes, loyalty is hard earned, but truly worth the investment and the wait.

The old ways of doing business are finished because customers themselves have changed. If you want to compete, you need to make sure your approach to buyers reflects this fact and reaches out to the consumer in a way that both builds value and instills trust in your business. Chasing business today is often a fruitless endeavor. Your energy should be focused on discovering ways you can be of further service to your existing customers, qualified prospective buyers, suppliers and anyone else in your circle of acquaintances.

Investing in this new currency is a serious time commitment, but remember that this initial intensive development of your network will enable you to put less time into marketing and hunting for prospective clients in the long run. It is those who recognize the value of connections and choose to actively cultivate them who will emerge as winners in the Trust & Value Economy. If you want to be successful in the modern market, you must be prepared to spend the time and do whatever else it takes to develop your network. Understand that, and you'll realize this is YOUR economy.

KEY TAKEAWAY

To win in the Trust & Value Economy, invest in building your network and further developing your connections. Connections are the new currency, the more powerful your network, the easier your sales process.

163

CHAPTER 13

Sell Small to Sell Big

Ah the weekly sales meeting! For most of your team this is the most dreaded meeting of the week. Why? Because we all know if we are not at the top of the highest performers, we are going to get a lecture and our faces rubbed in the success of our teammates. In the typical sales meeting, the sales manager and the leadership make a fuss over the top performers in the company. You will hear high praise for those who closed the most deals or sold the most products for the past month or quarter. These people are celebrated and rewarded with bonuses and other incentives. They are held up as examples for their ability to close deals, post high sales numbers, and sell a high number of products or services.

During these meetings, you will rarely hear the sales manager praising company representatives for their efforts to retain customers, deeply connect with customers, or for listening to prospects and discover their true needs. Many within the business world fail to see the important role that building relationships and trust plays in securing repeat customers and creating long-term, higher-value sales. It's unfortunate, because these are the key to long-lasting success in the Trust & Value Economy.

Sales goals have changed; the reward is in the relationship

Many of today's leaders are still leading their sales teams with out-dated and backward thinking sales techniques—techniques that may yield short-term results but are burning out their sales teams and their customers.

Many, but not Peter Krauss.

Peter is chief sales and marketing officer for Plasticard Logitech Inc. PLI is a company best known for making and distributing electronic key cards in a wide range of industries. Founded in the early 1990s, PLI has grown at rapid speed, reporting some of its strongest growth since the economic downturn. Hmmm, think about that; a company that works in hospitality (an industry hit hard by this economy) is experiencing consistent record growth. Peter joined PLI four years ago, and has taken the sales team to levels that even the board of directors doubted his ability to achieve.

Peter is confident and driven, to say the least. And within moments of meeting him, you know if you work with him you are either going to be successful or you are going to go somewhere else.

I first met Peter when I was asked to present at the PLI's annual sales rally. I arrived just in time to listen to Peter make his opening remarks. Much to my shock, he focused his talk on encouraging (really ordering) the team to stop selling. He went on to share that he did not want anyone on his entire sales team to spend their days with clients and prospects selling to those prospects and clients. As the team sat there a little confused waiting for the punch line, Peter went on to explain what he did want, and that was relationship builders.

He wanted his team to be proactive in connecting with customers, to be advocates for customers, and to be a team full of associates doing whatever it took to identify what the customer needed and deliver above those expectations. He definitely wanted them spending their days with clients and prospects, but what he also wanted was a long-term approach that would secure customers who were loyal, referred business, and would grow with PLI.

So, what were the results of his approach to the traditional sales meeting? What did he gain from praising those that invested in *the customer, who took the time to build a relationship with their prospects? When I showed up to speak at their sales rally a year later, they were in Peter's words, "going to the Super Bowl for the second time." Any football fan knows that is nearly impossible. In a struggling economy, in challenging times, in a company dedicated to a chaotic industry like hospitality, PLI has embraced the Trust & Value Economy and seen record growth and unprecedented sales.*

And where is PLI today? It is growing faster and stronger than ever. As this book goes to press, they are headed to the Super Bowl for the third time. Building trust and value works.

The sales funnel is now an hourglass

In the Trust & Value Economy, how we sell must change because the sales cycle has changed. The Trust & Value funnel looks more like an hourglass (see graphic) than a funnel. Moving a prospect to close takes far more investment of time and energy on the front end of the sale. Good follow-up and continued relationship building take investment after the first sale. Skills such as listening, questioning and connecting are critical at all times when working with prospects and customers.

Today's sales cycle has three major phases: awareness, sales, and loyalty. Handling each phase correctly and in order earns you the reward to move to the next phase. Move too fast through any one of these phases or move too fast through the sales hourglass and you will lose the prospect.

This takes patience and a more intuitive approach. To succeed, you still need to be aggressive and persistent, but that needs to be balanced with a strong dose of the soft skills. In the last ten years or so, we've lost our focus on and appreciation for the soft skills. Instead we have taken a far more pushy approach to sales, doggedly pursuing prospects under the guise of follow-up. Sales professionals describing themselves as aggressive and goal-focused have been the ones held in high regard. But fast forward to the Trust & Value Economy, and you will find those very same sales people struggling to close a deal. Why? Because today it takes a new type of sales person to close the deal, one who is "client-centric" not "me-centric." They have to be willing to spend even more time in the awareness phase of the calling process, investing in the prospect first. This economy is about giving and investing long before you can expect to receive.

It is highly unlikely that customers will make a purchase from a business that they know very little about and with whom they have no experience. Getting to the opportunity to close the big sale or establish a relationship that results in repeat business will take some time and might involve a "tester" sale.

Skilled sales people matter

What is this "tester" sale and where does it come from? The "tester" sale is a small sale that lets customers experience your company before investing in a big sale. In other words, you are selling small to sell big.

That first, small sale is best handled by a person skilled in selling in the Trust & Value Economy. Now, this is good news for sales people. This group of professionals has been subject to diminishing importance in the age of Internet shopping and objective customer reviews. But the art of developing relationships—i.e. selling—is a key competitive advantage in the Trust & Value Economy. So having knowledgeable, well-trained salespeople is a must.

A business owner or sales professional who really enjoys getting to know people and incrementally building trust—thus building sales—will thrive in this economy whether they are connecting at a brick-and-mortar location or via the web. Be aware that electronic media has not eliminated the need for relationship building; in fact it has enhanced it. Sales professionals are critical in making the sales process easier and more enjoyable for the prospect.

Now more than ever, prospects and customers want to interact. So skills such as answering questions, acting as a resource, being an advocate, and proactively suggesting ideas and solutions are incredibly valuable in a way that static promotional materials and even websites are not.

Sales grow with trust

As with any relationship, business connections start at a low level of trust and must go through a progression of steps to reach full confidence between client and company. For many businesses, this progression to gaining full confidence is a mystery they cannot seem to solve. How do you turn browsers into buyers who will feel comfortable enough to dig deep into their pockets to make a major purchase or repeatedly buy only from you?

The secret is surprisingly simple but requires commitment. Often, prospects don't immediately open up about their most pressing needs. And they are understandably reluctant to share those interests with someone they perceive as coming on too fast or as only interested in their own agenda. I mean you wouldn't share your problems with a pushy stranger, would you?

This is why you need to give the relationship time to develop and invest in it. Ask good, strong and logical questions that are connected with what they have already revealed. Be sure to pause and wait for the person you are speaking with to respond. Show you are paying close attention by asking follow-up questions, making sure that you are keeping the focus firmly on your prospect and the issues that he or she is facing.

If the potential buyer feels that you are leading them to a particular solution in order to make a specific sale rather than because you want to help them reach the best solution to their particular need, their trust may be broken. Your goal is not to swoop in and "sell" your prospect on an entire system that is going to solve all of his or her problems. If you jump the gun and try to push the prospect into making a decision too early in the relationship, you will lose out on the opportunity for the big sale or repeat business down the road.

Instead, take your conversations in bite-sized chunks. Focus on the smaller issues they are currently presenting even if you suspect that there is a larger need that they have yet to reveal. Sum up what your prospect has told you about the problem and ask them if you understand the issue correctly.

Now that you have their attention, ask if he or she would like to talk about an idea that you have for a solution. Since they are already engaged in the conversation and you have created an atmosphere of trust, your prospect will likely be open to listening to an idea.

Presenting a unique solution rather than a specific product or package system ensures that there is no pressure on the prospect to buy. Even if the prospect does not buy from you at that point (and he or she may well decide to make a purchase), you have established yourself as someone who is willing to carefully consider and offer solutions to whatever issues the prospect is facing. When your prospect is ready to buy, he or she will be much more likely to turn to you since you have already taken the time to listen and develop trust.

In a nutshell, here are the three biggest tips I can give you on how to sell successfully in the Trust & Value Economy.

1. **Connect with the right prospects** –Not everyone wants to do business with you and you do not want to do business with everyone (more on this in the next chapter). We are becoming a niche society, and you need to find your niche. Really get to know your customers and understand why they enjoy and benefit from doing business with you. Then use that information to choose your prospects. Selling only feels like selling when you are trying to get someone to buy something he or she really doesn't want. Selling feels like helping when you choose the right prospects.

2. **Help prospects understand value**—It makes me crazy when sales people ask, "How can I help you today." If I knew how your product or service could help me then why do I even need to talk with you? That is the power of a salesperson. You know your product or service. Your job is to help me understand how what you offer is going to make my life better. If you can do that, I am eager to buy!

3. **Be trustworthy**—Trust is a funny word in that it is hard to get your arms around. I mean how do you know if you are someone people trust? It is actually easy, just look at what people are saying about you; your current customers; the media; the prospects that

you have spoken with. If you are waiting until you meet someone to build trust, you are already behind the eight ball. You need to have established trust and credibility long before you ever knock on your prospect's door.

I will admit that selling is not easy in this economy, but it is simple. And you can be successful—very successful. More importantly, you can enjoy it. And I believe enjoy it more than ever before.

Begin by being yourself; treat your prospects just how you would want to be treated. We are living in the time of authenticity, trust and value. These are pretty good traits for any sales person or company to have and share with their clients. In this economy patience is a virtue and the need for instant gratification is a curse. This is a Trust & Value Economy. And trust takes time to build. Value takes time to understand. If you push your clients or prospects too hard and too fast, you'll lose.

Take the time to sell small and you will earn the right to sell big.

KEY TAKEAWAY

If you want to win in the Trust & Value Economy take a lesson from CEO Peter Krauss, and stop selling and start building relationships one step at a time.

CHAPTER 14

News Flash: Not Everyone Wants To Do Business With You

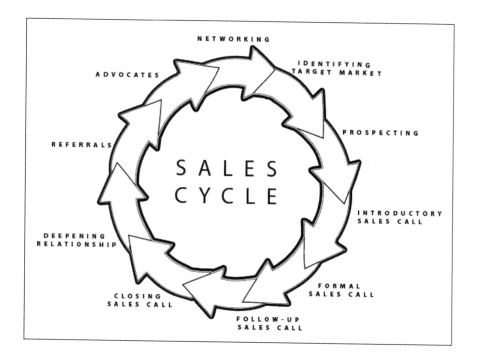

Generating revenue is the lifeblood of any business. Without revenue, you do not have a business. And revenue comes from sales. A standard sales cycle has a number of stages, which will usually include the following:

Identifying the target market

Networking

Prospecting

Introductory sales call

Formal sales call

Follow-up sales call

Closing sales call

Deepening relationship

Referrals

Advocates

As you can see, there are a lot of steps. And many you will repeat several times before you ever get to the close, referral or advocate state. So going through these steps with multiple prospects is very time-consuming. Working through the process without appreciable results can be costly for your company, as well as a demoralizing experience for you and your sales team.

In fact, do this enough times without results and sales professionals just give up. I think more than any other time since I have been in business, these days I have experienced more sales professionals burned out, tired and just plain feeling the stress of the pressure to reach their goals.

In addition, just to add insult to injury, this economy has made this process much longer. In a strong economy, it can take three or four touches to close a deal. In a tough economy, that number jumps to six or eight. And in a shifting economy like this one, that number has moved to from twelve to sixteen. Shifting means uncertainty, and uncertainty slows the decision-making process down.

Now, you can go broke having to call on every single customer twelve to sixteen times. So if you want to succeed in this economy, you need to shorten the sales cycle.

Choose your prospects well

Here's the big secret to a shorter sales cycle: choose the right prospect in the first place. The better you identify your prospects, the better you know your prospects, the shorter your sales cycle will be.

As a business leader, you want to keep your sales team motivated and inspired. To do that, you need to make the sales process fun as well as effective. To do that, you need to ensure that you and your sales force are spending time interacting with more qualified prospects.

Here is a news flash—not everyone wants to do business with you! Here is another news flash—you do not want to do business with everyone! You already know who your best customer is; now use that information to choose your prospects more wisely and better.

You know who you enjoy doing business with and who enjoys doing business with you. You know what type of individual really benefits from working with a company like yours, and which does not. So use that information to choose your prospects, and make the selling and growth process better for you.

A few years ago I was speaking at an event in Atlanta, Georgia. It was a CEO roundtable, and we had 60 CEOs in the room. I was the last speaker of the day, the only thing standing between them and cocktails.

As I finished my presentation, one of the CEOs asked to speak with me after. He was energetic, smart, very type A—my favorite type of prospect. As we walked into happy hour, he shared that he would really like to have me come to his company and work with his sales team. They wanted to go next level, and they knew they would need help. He shared that he had spoken with the team, they were on board, and that he would like to be involved.

I could not believe my ears. This was unbelievable. Here, right before my eyes was an amazing prospect, great company and with a committed team ready to get started. On the outside, he looked like the perfect prospect. All systems go!

However, just to be sure, I asked a few more questions. What challenges has he faced in the past with the sales team? Where does he see opportunity? What is the competition like? Where do you see the company in the next five years? His answers were smack on target. This was moving forward, and I was getting excited.

Then I asked, why are you not achieving the results you want right now, what is in the way? He responded that last year his brother-in-law had come to work for him, and he put him over the sales team. Since he was family, he felt he needed to give his brother-in-law a leadership role. The challenge was that the brother-in-law was not only ineffective, he was lazy, and he was overpaid. The team knew it, and it was killing morale. So, I asked what he had tried to do to fix the situation. He gave me a long list, and he said honestly there is not much left to try. I was hoping you would have some answers. I asked if he had thought about demoting him or replacing him.

The CEO just laughed. He said, "Meridith, I do not think you understand. I have been happily married for more than 20 years, and I plan to stay happily married for another 20. There is no way I can touch my brother-in-law."

Well, sad as it was, I knew in that moment that this was not a good prospect for me. Could I have fixed that situation? Maybe. But most likely not. I certainly would not have made any profit or really have satisfied my customer. I had 59 other CEOs in that room, 59 other prospects with the hope of a shorter sales cycle. I quickly learned that I needed to leave this prospect (no worries, I connected him to a great peer of mine who is a turn-around expert) and move on to find a prospect that was a better fit.

Choosing your prospects carefully will make all the difference in your ability to shorten and, quite frankly, enjoy the sales cycle.

Develop a targeted customer/client wish list

So how do you identify the best prospects?

Begin with your best customers. Literally, make a list of your best 20 customers. By best, I mean those you enjoy working with, those who pay you, those for whom price is not an issue, those who refer you business, those who use—really use—your products and services, and those who have benefited from the depth of your services.

Once you make that list, review it. And then take a closer look. You will start to see themes and things that these clients have in common. Characteristics such as age, length of time with the business, size of the business, particular industry, geographic location, personality types, hobbies, etc. Those themes, those things your best customers have in common, are the characteristics and traits you are looking for in the prospects you want. Match the themes of your best customers to the prospects (future customers) you are calling on, and watch your sales cycle shorten.

After three years in business, I started noticing a pattern (themes) with my favorite clients. The clients I most loved and gained energy from working with shared some very key traits. They were all type A personalities—often my meetings with them were at six or seven in the morning. They were new in their roles, either having just joined the company or recently been promoted, usually there just under two years. Their companies were in growth mode and faced several major opportunities and the challenges that come with those. They had a desire to both develop internal talent and acquire competitors. Everyone held either senior level positions or was the CEO of the company. They were a strong combination of confident and humble, serious drive and great self-reflection, and outspoken, saying what they wanted but with a great ability to laugh at themselves. And, a bonus for me, all had a terrific sense of humor. They were mostly between the ages of 45 and 60, very athletic and active, and family men. Yes, at this time, most were men.

Looking at that list, I matched what I saw there with my prospect list and I saw a disconnect. I saw that often I was not calling on decision makers with those qualities and traits. No wonder all of a sudden I was struggling to close business. In addition, I found it curious that I was not working with more professional women.

Armed with this information, I was able to both rebuild my prospect list and adjust my strategy to call on prospects that would more readily be open to my ideas and the product my company offered. In addition, with a prospect list full of the type of people I enjoy working with, making sales calls was about to become a whole lot more fun. And today, I am happy to say my client list is about 50 percent women and 50 percent men. I like the healthy balance for my clients and for my personal growth.

Research is critical when it comes to both building and knowing your prospects. The more closely a prospective client matches your customer wish list, the more likely that person or company is to buy what your company offers. Invest and take the time to qualify a prospect against the criteria you have developed. It is well worth the tedious step it feels like. It is the essential part of the sales process that truly results in greater efficiency and productivity.

In reality, taking a little time on the front end will put you in the power position when it comes to building your prospect list. With little effort, you will discover whether or not a company or individual is a good prospect and who exactly will want to do business with you. The concept is simple—the more you focus your energy on getting appointments with qualified prospects, the shorter your sales cycle will be. In fact, it will be much shorter than if you started from a general list of prospects who may or may not be a good fit for what you have to offer.

Let the conversation begin

Did you notice that I didn't say, "a good fit for what you are trying to sell"? Your goal should not be to "sell" the prospect, but rather to start a conversation about a related problem or concern the prospect is currently experiencing. If you have done your homework thoroughly, you will not need to "convince" the prospective buyer of their need for your product. You will be able to simply help them uncover an existing problem or need and then help them create solutions and opportunities. Prospects are not really interested in dealing with someone who is trying to sell them something, but they are very interested in working with a sales professional who is interested in them and committed to finding solutions that will clearly benefit them.

To a number of people, "selling" is a word that implies persuading someone to buy something they may not really want or need—using a lot of pressure and hype to do so. Taking the time to determine whether or not a potential client is a well-qualified prospect can make a major difference in both your productivity and your selling experience. When you offer solutions that make sense to qualified prospects, the sales naturally fall into place. Rather than being perceived as a pesky salesperson, you will be able to position yourself as a helpful asset partnering with the company or person to promote their future success or prevent future problems.

Making sure that you are marketing your products and services to the most qualified prospects can also help to establish your credibility as a business committed to the needs of the consumer. By targeting only potential customers with an actual, demonstrable need for your services, you will gain a reputation for offering quality products rather than trying to make a quick sale. And when consumers perceive you as a partner in meeting their needs, they will be more likely to refer your company to other members of their business or personal community. You become a company worth talking about.

KEY TAKEAWAY

To win in the Trust & Value Economy, shorten the sales cycle by choosing appropriate prospects.

CHAPTER 15

Sell Opportunity—Become a Partner and an Advocate

As a business owner or sales professional in the Trust & Value Economy, your challenge is to establish your reputation and that of your business as a partner and an advocate for your customers, with an overall driving mission of helping your customers improve their lives.

Now, your ability to help improve a person's life depends largely on your understanding of their definition of a "better life." For some potential customers, a better life depends on finding ways to save time and/or money. Other customers may believe that operating their business in a morally and environmentally responsible manner is an essential part of living a better life. It does not matter what their definition of success is, your job as the sales professional is to deeply understand that definition, so you can help them identify products and services that can support them in their efforts to achieve their dreams. Help them to see the opportunities that your products or services can bring or open for them.

Begin as an advocate

You see as sales professionals and business owners, it is *our* job—not our prospects' and not our customers'—to know the range of products and services we offer, as well as all the benefits, advantages and ways in which those products and services can enhance our prospects' and customers' lives. That is our job.

The reason we invest in getting to know our customers is so we can understand what they need now as well as in the future. Their role is to share their story with us (and if we have built trust they will do that). And once we understand their story, we can take everything we hear and everything we learn and match it to the products and services that we offer, the products and service that we know will help our customers on their journey to achieving their dreams.

I am old enough that I was working in the time of pre-call planning. When I think about that now it makes me laugh. For those of you who never used extensive pre-call planning tools, let me share the details.

The idea was we would sit down and brainstorm with another calling officer about how the sales call should go. What we assumed the prospect needed, what questions we would ask, and then what products or services we would offer and how we would close the deal. The products and services we would offer would be our goal, the result we wanted, the way in which we would know we made a good call.

How ridiculous is that? To design a conversation and the products and services that are right for your prospects or customers before you have even talked with them and without involving them. That strategy in this economy will not work.

As you know by this point, in this economy as opposed to the old economy, there is a massive difference in the type of relationship you need to have with your clients. In the old economy, that call-strategy worked because if you only sold your customer a few products or services and they left without all of their needs realized or fulfilled, there was a good chance they would still remain your customer. Due to low competition and a push economy, going for quantity versus quality and developing lots of relationships instead of deep relationships was a perfectly acceptable way to do business. And it was a profitable way to do business. In this economy, the Trust & Value Economy, it is not.

Today, you have put so much time, energy and expense into building the relationship, you want to reap the most rewards possible. The hardest part of selling is getting to that first sale. So when you get there, you need to go as deep as possible.

In addition, customers expect more. They are giving you their business; if you have other products or services that will save them time or make them money, they expect you to let them know.

If you do not take the initiative to really become an advocate for your customers, someone else will. Competition is unbelievably high. So not showing customers what else they can do, how they can grow and develop with your organization, is an invitation to ask them to take their business somewhere else. And, believe me, they will.

As we have discussed, listening to your customers is a top priority in this economy. When you listen, your customers will share their stories, their dreams, their challenges and their opportunities. They will tell you everything you want to know and more about their businesses. Your role at that point is to take in everything you have heard, and begin to think about what you can do, what you can offer, to help them achieve their goals.

That is selling opportunity, and at this point you have earned the right. You have established the relationship, built the trust, invested in them. Believe me they are ready and want to be sold.

Sit on the same side of the table

Once they are ready, if you don't start selling opportunity, you will shatter the trust you have built. Oh, your customers will still like you, but they will no longer value you as a trusted member of their team who is proactively looking for ways to move their business forward.

Getting to know what your clients value is the key. Considering ways in which the services or products provided by your company meet those needs allows you to present yourself as an asset in your customers' goal of achieving their long-term objectives. This is when you stop seeing your business as something completely separate from theirs. You make a shift in attitude. This shift enables you to creatively design ways in which you can enter into a partnership with your customers.

This drastic shift in attitude requires a shift in your own paradigm, an overhaul of the way you think about sales and prospective clients. And it will pay off exponentially in your business dealings.

If you continue to maintain a provider-customer mentality, you will be forever stuck on the opposite side of the table from prospective business associates. No matter how much posturing you do, as long as you are on opposite sides of the table—with the sale between you—prospective clients will never be able to view you as a trusted partner with the best interests of their company at heart.

A much better strategy is to enter into a relationship with your customer where you can be on the same side of the table, as partners who are working toward the same goals. Never forget that your customers' ability to continue using your products or services depends on the continued success of their business. That thought alone should be all you need to shift your mindset to see your customers as partners.

Grow into a trusted partner

As a partner, the benefit you bring to your customers is that with you they will be able to reach their goals more quickly and easily. Whether you are providing the event planning for a Fortune 500's largest convention, expanding a new product line, or simply helping a woman find the perfect dress in your shop to wear to her daughter's wedding, if your attitude and performance show commitment to their success, the client will remember that connection and come back to you the next time they have a need.

You will experience lasting benefits from this simple attitude adjustment to partnering, since it fosters loyalty on the part of your customer toward you and you toward your customer. Your services or products may be essentially the same as many of your competitors, but your attitude and actions in presenting them will make a huge difference in how your clients perceive them.

For example, do you seem genuinely and authentically interested in helping them achieve what they want? Do you bring ideas or solutions to the table? Can you open their eyes to possibilities that move them closer to their goals? Do you challenge them and push them out of their comfort zone? That is the difference a partner can make.

It's relatively easy for a customer to end a relationship with a business in which it hasn't invested a lot of time. If you have done the legwork to establish a trust-based business relationship with your customers, however, it is much more likely to be a long-lasting and beneficial one for both of you.

Since you have taken the time to get to know your customers—what they hope to accomplish, the specific parameters they are working with and the values that are most important to them—you are in a unique position to guide them toward the products and services best suited to their needs.

In the example of helping find the most appropriate dress for the mother of the bride to wear to a wedding, asking simple questions about what she hopes for that day, what the bride and groom are envisioning, and even how she always dreamed this day would look open the conversation and build trust. In addition, you may ask about the wedding colors, the time of the wedding and the location. All of this will go a long way towards convincing the customer that you are invested in getting her exactly what she needs.

Create a relationship of mutual benefit

Showing interest in their specific needs reassures potential clients that you are not merely looking to complete a sale but to make sure the arrangement is working well for both of you. This may mean offering your customer a referral to another provider when the situation calls for it. Though it may seem counterintuitive to send a customer elsewhere even when your product or service is not the best fit for them, the gesture will establish your credibility as a partner in their goals rather than as a self-interested seller.

When you step away from focusing on "selling" to your customer and instead see your customer as part of a network that works to advance you both, you will recognize the benefits of keeping his or her best interests in mind. Even if your business is not a good fit for a customer's particular need or goal, there will probably be other situations for which you will be a better match in the future.

Once the customer begins to view your company as a partner in their goals, they will be likely to come to you as a resource for business needs. The fear of missing out on even a single selling opportunity is only valid if you believed that you get only one chance to work with the customers who are in your network. If, however, you treat your business relationship as long-term partnerships, you will have as many opportunities to work with them as you create for yourself by being a great partner and advocate.

Be a partner and an advocate to your team

Being good at sales, partnering with your customers, is about more than just being a good sales professional. As a business owner, sales manager or peer, you need to be a partner and an advocate for your sales team.

So, ask yourself how good is your sales team, your individual sales performers? Are they exceeding expectations, are they surpassing their goals by third quarter, and deepening and retaining client relationships? Well, if you are like most sales leaders trying to lead in today's challenging economy, the answer to that question is "well sort of". You have one of those sales teams where you have a few shining stars, a few middle of the road performers, and too many stragglers that just seem unable to get near, let alone, reach their goals.

If that describes you or your sales team, trust me, you are not alone. A few weeks ago, I was working with a client, Tom, in Denver, Colorado. He's a sales leader, in fact one of the top performers in the insurance industry, and a sales leader with three exceptional team members, two middle of the road performers, and three, yes count them three, team members that have not made their numbers since the market started to turn. Tom, heard me speak at an Insurance Convention, and hired me to come in and work one-on-one with his three struggling performers. For me, this was a great job, right up my alley, as I love and am passionate about helping people achieve their potential. So, just like I always do, I began this coaching engagement with an intake session with Tom, the struggling performers, as well as the other members of the team. What I found out, while not all that surprising, was about to change the course of this coaching engagement. You see, what I found out was there was very little, if any, true sales leadership going on with this team. The team had their goals, they had their reports they were required to fill out, and they had their regular sales meetings, and annual reviews, but as for true sales leadership it was pretty much null and void. That information, just that knowledge, told me as a sales coach, that my job was not to focus on improving the performance of the sales team, but rather to focus on improving the performance of the sales leader.

If you are a sales leader who wants to increase the performance of your team then understand it begins with you. Your first step is to turn around and take a long, hard look in the mirror; because trust me, the skills and ability of your team, every member of your team, are directly related to your ability and skill as a sales leader.

Ouch right? Yep, ouch! It is true, if you want to increase their performance, if you want your team to up their game, then you need to up yours. The very definition of leadership is to influence, support and help a group of people to achieve a goal. Note, the definition is not to oversee and watch while a few people achieve the goal, and to yell at all the others to just work harder. Yet all too often that is how we lead our sales teams, taking credit for those who succeed and taking none for those who do not.

So you think that you are a sales leader? Well, take a moment and put yourself to the test. Get honest and put yourself through the paces of what an effective sales leader really looks like and what they really do. Then ask yourself if you measure up.

1. **Create the future**—effective sales leaders first and foremost have a vision. They know where they are going, and they have a plan to get there. Beyond that, effective sales leaders ensure that the plan includes each and every member of their team, and a road map of how to get there.

2. **Paint the picture**—armed with a vision and a plan, effective sales leaders are able to share that vision in a way that paints a very clear picture for everyone. In addition, effective sales leaders have a strategy to communicate that plan clearly and consistently so that every member of the team is able to see what their leader sees, imagine what they imagine, and understand their personal impact on that vision

3. **Move the Masses**—effective sales leaders invest the time to motivate inspire and share the passion with their team. They

embrace the small stuff, the soft skills, and understand the importance of infusing energy into their teams on a consistent basis. They understand that helping people to reach their potential is about more than learning new skills, and doing the work, it is about having someone to encourage, support and say thank you and get excited about every inch of progress they make along the way.

4. **Walk The Talk**—The ability to actually do the job is at the top of the list of every effective sales leader. Now no worries, I did not say you had to be the best at the job or even still require yourself to do the job day in and day out, but if you expect to be an effective sales leader, you have to role model the job you want and expect your team to do. You have to be willing, and be able to prove, yes, prove, you are and can do what you are asking them to do.

5. **Speak Softly**—An effective sales leaders understands not only the importance of, but the real meaning of, accountability. They use accountability as a learning tool, not a punishment tool. A word that is often both misunderstood and administered incorrectly by sales managers, accountability is all too often used as a way to identify and catch someone doing something wrong. Instead accountability should be used as tool to both reward behavior done right, and identify where team members need help and support to improve. Effective sales leaders use accountability as a tool to understand if their team members need skill development, process instructions or just a good 'ole attitude adjustment to improve their performance and take ownership for their success.

6. **Do The Work**—top of the list for any effective sales leader is the understanding of how incredibly important it is to invest

in yourself. Great sales leaders are constant learners, dedicated to increasing their own knowledge and expanding their own skills, not only so they improve, but so they are in a position to better improve the performance of their team members. Reading industry publications, attending conferences, participating in webinars, and working with their own sales coach, are all at the top of the list for effective sales leaders.

7. **Rip The Band-Aid**—to be effective strong sales leaders know it is better to deal with things head on, efficiently and directly, rather than let them simmer. Avoiding problems and confrontations only turns mole hills into mountains. Dealing with issues and people directly and honestly, is something effective sales leaders do to prevent small problems from become big ones, earn the respect of their peers, and ensure the energy of the team stays focused on the client not on the office drama.

8. **Open Doors**—last, but certainly not least, the effective sales leader actually leads. They show their team members the way by teaching, sharing, educating and engaging them in the learning process. Fueled by their own passion for knowledge, they share that knowledge and inspire that level of educational desire in their teams.

Leading in today's environment I will admit is not easy, but it is simple. You have to want to lead a team to be effective at leading a team. You have to be more interested in your team's success than your own. Most importantly, you have to be willing to take a long, hard look in the mirror when any or every member of the team is not succeeding and ask yourself who really is not reaching their goals? Then take the steps you need to take to become the leader we know you all have the ability to be!

KEY TAKEAWAY

To win in the Trust & Value Economy become a partner and an advocate, someone your customers can count on to proactively "sell" them new ideas, strategies and solutions that will ensure their success.

CHAPTER 16

Overfill Your Sales Funnel

As we've discussed, the sales cycle—the time it takes to have a sale go from start to close—takes longer than it used to. Closing a sale these days, or should I say waiting for a sale to close these days, is one of the most stressful experiences sales professionals working in today's market go through. It is the ultimate test of patience, something that does not come easily to a business owner, sales professional or CEO. But it is just a fact in tough and shifting economic times that sales cycles slow down.

In the Trust & Value Economy, if you have not adjusted your sales process, the sales cycle can feel like it has stopped. Remember that today the customer, not you, is in complete control of the buying cycle. Now don't worry, this does not put you in a position where you just have to take anything that comes along. As we discussed in previous chapters, you may not be in control, but you still have some power. But your customer cannot be pushed.

Fill 'er up

Now, a slow sales cycle combined with a customer you can't push and one who is in ultimate control of the buying cycle can make for a less than free-flowing sales pipeline and cause a stressed crew of sales professionals. That is true unless you do one thing, one simple idea that is as plain as the nose on your face—overfill your sales funnel.

You need to have your sales funnel so full, have it so fat with prospects, that you are almost relieved when a prospect needs more time or slows the cycle down. (Okay, that may be an exaggeration, but you get the idea.)

Do you know the hardest and most difficult time to close a sale? The most difficult time to close a sale is when you need the sale to close, of course. You can pretty much guarantee the moment you need that sale to close to meet budget, meet a goal or whatever, that Murphy's Law will rear its ugly head and the sale will not close. Something will happen out of left field and derail all of your hard work.

The moment that sale becomes more about your need than about the need of your prospect or customer is the moment the sale goes off kilter and things start to go wrong.

Buying after all, remember, is emotional. In the Trust & Value Economy, customers are more emotional than ever. They can sense, no matter what the sales person is saying, whether the sales professional is more interested in closing the sale or in helping them achieve their gaols. They can feel it when you need that sale to close. And the moment they feel that your need to close the sale is more important than their need to have a choice, that's the moment you lose the sale. The moment you become needy, they know it. And they move on.

Sell like you don't need the sale

To win in the Trust & Value Economy, sell from a place of power. Believe that while you do want to help the customer, you do not need the sale.

Whoa! Not need a sale! In this tough economy? Yes, you need to be selling and growing your business or portfolio with such fluidity that if one sale does not happen, it is not a problem as you have another right around the corner.

You see, the moment you don't need your sales to close is the moment more sales will start closing. It's sort of like dating, remember that? If you needed a date for Friday night, you couldn't get one even if your life depended on it. Start dating someone, and the dates start coming out of the woodwork. I don't know why this happens but we are creatures of energy and when we are in a place of power and radiating confidence, people feel it and they want to be connected.

The only way to sell from a place of power is to have so many prospects and opportunities moving through your pipeline that you don't sweat the occasional delay or even "no" response from a customer. You have the breathing room to not panic when a prospect calls and moves a meeting, or they need more time to make a decision. Instead of taking it as a personal attack, you simply listen to what your prospect or customer shares (imagine that) and realize you can use this time to continue to build the relationship with them and add even more value.

Plus, now you can turn your attention to the endless stream of other prospects and customers coming through your pipeline as one or several of those are sure to continue moving forward and ultimately close.

Again, in a Trust & Value Economy, you need to understand that a slow sales cycle is just your reality and the more desperate you are, the more invested you are in just a few clients, the more stressful and unsuccessful you are going to be.

One critical mistake I see many sales professionals make is to focus too much on landing the "big sale." They invest too much of their time and effort on trying to encourage a few high-dollar prospects to make the decision to buy. While one sale at this level may have the potential to put the company in a good financial position for a while or help a sales professional exceed a few months' worth of goals, what happens if the prospect they are counting on does not make the decision to buy? When you put all (or most) of your eggs in one basket, you run the very real risk of working incredibly hard for no return on investment or worse yet having cash flow issues that can have a detrimental impact on the rest of your business.

In a shifting economy, where so much can happen and so much can change at a moment's notice, investing in too few prospects can put your company in serious jeopardy.

When you have so much riding on a few sales, maintaining focus on the needs of the potential buyer can be incredibly difficult. You may find yourself unintentionally putting pressure on the customer to purchase now or before they are ready. And by now we know that pushing your prospect in the Trust & Value Economy is a sure fire way to lose the sale. Even if the person was seriously thinking about making a purchase, your intensity in trying to close the sale may raise their suspicions about the quality of the product or the integrity of your company. At the very least, it makes them feel unheard and uncared about.

I was doing some volunteer work for a non-profit. My role was to be in charge of the marketing and promotion budget. We had a huge event coming up, and we had a good-sized budget to invest in advertising and market. The money had been donated to our organization and earmarked for marketing. As soon as the local radio and television advertising representatives found out about the budget, they jumped all over us.

Well, I was curious to find out what opportunities there was out there in radio and TV, so I invested the time to sit down and talk with many of them. I informed each one that I would be making no decision until the first of the year (the event was scheduled for the summer of the following year), and I wanted to put together a budget, set some goals, and get everything approved by the board.

For the most part, everyone was respectful. However this one television station kept calling, kept throwing me ideas, and kept giving me small ways I could get started. Now I will have to admit some of the ideas were good, but it drove me nuts. It was so clear that the representative did not listen or did not care what I said. And I cannot tell you how that affected me. The entire experience felt so much more about her than it felt about me, that when it came time to put the project together, I left her organization out completely. All because she pushed the sale rather than trying to influence it.

You see buyers are well aware that they always have other options available to them, and they will weigh them very carefully before committing to a purchase. Remember, this is a Trust & Value Economy. When you start applying pressure or you seem less than confident, then you start laying the groundwork to undo all of the trust you spent so much time and energy building.

Take the high road and stay on it

Since you have limited influence over the speed or success of the sales cycle on any given purchase, your only remaining option is to keep your sales pipeline full, in fact overfilled, at all times. While depth of trust is important in your business relationships, it is also important to continually seek to broaden your network of potential clients. Use the information you learned in previous chapters to identify and pursue qualified prospects with a wide range of projects or purchase-size needs. If you keep your company in a position where you have multiple opportunities in various stages of development and sales are closing often, you no longer feel the pressure or need to be concerned about whether one or two major customers are going to make or break your year.

The decreased levels of pressure you feel will translate into the comfortable atmosphere that is essential for creating a trust-based relationship with all of your potential clients. And that decreased level of pressure will make your prospects and customers more comfortable as well, creating an environment that breeds sales and breeds success. The more relaxed you are, the better you are able to listen to the other people and express genuine interest in what they are saying about the challenges they are facing in their business.

It's much easier to step into the role of partner and advocate if you are not listening to an internal dialogue that reminds you, "I have to make this sale," over and over again. So cast your net as wide as you can when looking for opportunities to grow your business. Be open to staying in the awareness phase of the relationship as long as it takes, as long as your potential client wants and needs to stay there. Be generous when giving referrals to other organizations that may be a better fit for a prospect's needs. Your prospect and the business receiving the referral will appreciate your willingness to go the extra mile to meet the needs of the client when there is no apparent benefit to your company.

This is an economy where being authentic, doing the right thing, and taking the high road pays off and offers a more than generous return on investment.

When you do make a sale, you want to make sure you are doing so from a position of power instead of one of need. By always having a wide variety of prospects in various stages of the sales cycle, you can give your company the financial stability to focus on what you have to offer. As you present your products and services as valuable commodities with plenty of other prospective buyers, customers will be increasingly eager to do business with your company. In a Trust & Value Economy, you are embracing an entire lifestyle instead of an isolated effort to grow your business. Selling this way makes sales fun, easy and incredibly effective.

KEY TAKEAWAY

To win in the Trust & Value Economy, keep a healthy, fat sales pipeline so you sell from a place of power rather than a place of need.

CHAPTER 17

Yes, You Can Succeed in This New Economy

One morning, as I was listening to the news, the anchor began reporting about a veteran, a young soldier who had lost his leg, and was training for a climb, the climb of his life.

The reporter explained that the soldier was an elite Marine from New York whose leg had been destroyed by an IED attack in Iraq and later had to be amputated. The Marine, now wearing a prosthetic, was attempting to climb, yes climb, one of the steepest, most dangerous routes on icy Mount Washington, the highest peak on the East coast.

The reporter shared that this ascent was a way for this Marine to honor his fellow soldiers who did not make it back from Iraq. In addition, his hope was to use this climb to raise awareness and funds for the Special Operations Warrior Foundation, an organization that supports wounded and hospitalized soldiers and the children of those killed in combat.

The Marine, who was just 26, admitted that while the IED may have ended his career in the Marines, it had not stripped him of the "determination, perseverance and mental toughness I've gained". The anchor went on to tell this Marine's history; all that he had *gone through on the battlefield, in the hospital recovering from his injuries, and then the loss of his leg. Yet, despite all of that, against all the odds, he was still continuing to add to his amazing list of achievements. His story, as you can imagine, is nothing short of remarkable.*

While I was moved by his story, I was far more inspired by his words and his actions. The powerful message that he was conveying: that no matter what happened to him, what challenges, obstacles or insurmountable odds lay in his path, he was not going to be defeated. His attitude, his mental toughness, got me thinking about how much we are really capable of overcoming and of doing when we set our minds to it. And the impact that kind of attitude can have on the people who come in contact with it.

Get in shape now

So as you look at your future, and you begin to set your goals, define your focus, and get ready to take action, think about your attitude. Ask yourself, how mentally tough are you? Are you ready, mentally, for the Trust & Value Economy? Are you prepared to be flexible and responsive to your customers' ever changing needs and the new competition that is certain to come your way? Do you have the courage to take risks and try new things? And are you resilient enough to get back up after you fall? Because you will fall, make mistakes and make some bad decisions—we all will.

Trust me, how prepared you are, how mentally tough, has a direct impact on your success. So how do you get ready? How do you know if you have what it takes? Are there exercises, ideas and things you can do to get your mind and your attitude in shape? Absolutely!

Here are six techniques that I like to follow. Six ways I personally use to keep my attitude positive and my mental state strong no matter what the world throws at me:

1. **Embrace failure**—We have all heard it said that if you are not failing enough, you are not taking enough chances. And in my opinion you are missing opportunity. Failure unfortunately is something that our culture does not accept or have much use for anymore. So we have lost sight of one of our greatest learning tools. Understanding why something did not work is as important, if not more so, than learning how to make it work. Embrace failure as a learning tool, and consistently ask yourself these questions: What went well? What did not? What do I need to do differently going forward? Let go of your ego, learn from your mistakes, and failure will become a way to propel you forward.

2. **Forget outcomes**—You have far more control over the process than you do the outcome, so focus your attention there. Especially in today's economy with so many outside forces that can positively or negatively impact your success, your goals and expectations need to be flexible. Put your time and your energy into perfecting your process, delivering a better product, improving your sales strategy and actions, etc. Become the best at what you do and how you deliver it. A strong process will put you in position to be flexible, responsive to market changes, and give you the courage to take risks no matter what this Trust & Value Economy has in store for you.

3. **Take action**—Just do it, as Nike would say! Every single day, every single week, move forward and take action. With your process firmly in place, work it. Make the sales calls you said you would, coach your employees, follow up on customer service requests etc. In the Trust & Value Economy, those CEOs, business owners

and professionals who are achieving success are no smarter or more capable than you are—they are just taking action. Lots of people talk about what they are going to do, but few actually do it. Be among those who take action!

4. **Hang with the right people**—If you are going to succeed, if you are going to achieve a high level of mental toughness, then you need to surround yourself with people who support your goals and your attempts to make them happen. All too often I see professionals who get beaten down by bosses who focus on their mistakes and forget to point out what these professionals do well. Or they have family members and friends who seem to only see their mistakes as failures rather than learning opportunities. If you want to master this Trust & Value Economy and increase your mental toughness, then learn to set boundaries. Limit your time with people who do not infuse you with energy and increase your time with those that do. Remember, people who point out what you do wrong more than what you do right are people you need to limit your exposure to.

5. **Manage your energy**—So many of us have tried time and time again to manage our time with no luck at all. That is because time is not really the problem, the challenge is the amount of energy we have to accomplish everything we need and want to accomplish. The concept is simple really. There are people and things we choose to engage with that infuse us with energy, and people and things that deplete our energy. Our job is to learn to balance the two. Some things that deplete our energy can honestly be eliminated from our lives. Things like certain chores or social outings or business functions we attend. Then there are things that increase our energy, things such as our hobbies, certain business functions and people who make us laugh. Your job is to

make better choices and schedule your day around energy, not time. Certainly, we cannot get rid of everything that depletes our energy. But if you look at it honestly, there are definitely some energy-depleters that you can limit. In addition, and probably a more powerful exercise, identify what puts energy into your life and add more of that. For those days when you have to do tasks that deplete your energy, throw in a few energizers.

6. **Take personal responsibility**—My personal favorite. If you want to increase your mental toughness and learn to overcome obstacles and achieve great things in the Trust & Value Economy, then stop blaming other people or situations. Understand that everything that goes wrong or right in your life you had a hand in, and you are responsible for. So take a look at your actions, your behaviors and embrace your responsibility for the outcome. Understand this clearly, achieving success and taking personal responsibility are deeply connected. And one cannot, I repeat cannot, be achieved without the other.

Whatever we want to accomplish—even in the Trust & Value Economy—we can if we have the mental toughness to do so. I trust that few, if any of us, will face the challenges that young Marine faced. So if he can do it, if he can achieve his dreams, then we can too.

KEY TAKEAWAY

To win in the Trust & Value Economy, develop mental toughness and know you are capable of reaching your goals whatever obstacles are put in your path.

CHAPTER 18

What's Next

Who knows? There, I said it. Quite frankly I could end this book by saying nothing more than that.

Who knows what is next. The experts don't know. And the economists certainly don't know. So to win and to succeed in this economy, we all need to find comfort in the great unknown.

The one thing that is certain is that the Trust & Value Economy requires a different approach to business, one that is focused solely on the customer and places value on innovation and gets you comfortable in how to succeed in an environment where you have no clue what is coming next. The most positive way to receive this new business model is to embrace it for what it is—a new way of doing business—because believe me this model is here to stay. In this new world, things are moving, moving fast, and are in constant motion. If the last few years have taught us anything, it is that the one thing, the only thing, you can count on in this economy is inconsistency.

Despite the negative connotation that word bears, I consider this fact of the Trust & Value Economy to be a promising one. There is a certain sense of adventure that drives the best business owners and professionals. An owner who is prepared for and open to this new economy can actually come out stronger and can see this economy as full of opportunity. I mean *full of opportunity*.

So what are your next steps? Where do you go from here? Well, first make sure you embrace the new reality and you understand the fundamentals:

- Times have changed

- Competition is at an all time high

- Technology has changed everything

- And your customers are fully in control of the buying cycle. (No matter how you cut it, you are no longer driving, you are simply along for the ride, and the better you are at being the navigator the more successful you are going to be.)

Being good at what you do, offering a quality product or service is no longer good enough; it is simply your ticket to entry. You have to up your sales game, stand out and get above the white noise. You have to be focused. This new economy has brought forth a new customer—one that is more knowledgeable, more empowered and harder to win. With more competitors nipping at your heels, and customers overwhelmed with choice, you need to be at the top of your game, running on all cylinders to even get a shot at winning in this economy.

The most important skills you can possess as a sales professional or business owner today are focus, patience, listening and execution. Those skills will ensure you deliver trust and value to your customers and prospects. Understand that you are in this for the long haul. This economy is about hard work. There is no easier answer and certainly no instant gratification.

212

The strategies discussed in this book can help you to manage inconsistency. It is possible to take changes in your stride by developing security through long-term healthy relationships with the people who make up your business and professional network. If you have cultivated an extensive network of clients and prospects with whom you are constantly seeking ways to develop beneficial partnerships, the sudden dips and surges in the market will have far less drastic effects on your company.

Consumers know that they have more options than ever before when it comes to where and how they will buy the products and services they need. In fact, the sheer number of options may be overwhelming as clients consider starting the sales cycle with a company. That is why developing trust with prospects in everyday interactions, even those that are not directly related to sales, is such a vital part of growing your business.

Once you have earned their trust, you are likely to have a loyal customer who will continue to return to your company whenever they have a need related to what you offer (as long as you continue to operate in a trustworthy manner and provide real value in your business dealings). This shifted mindset, which views interaction with prospects as part of building a long-term business relationship rather than as a one-time chance to close a sale, is the real meaning of the Trust & Value Economy. So, welcome to the Trust & Value Economy!

KEY TAKEAWAY

The Trust & Value Economy is your economy; now go out there and get it!